War in Paradise

Stories of World War II in Florida

Eliot Kleinberg

Copyright © 1999
The Florida Historical Society Press
435 Brevard Avenue
Cocoa, FL 32922

ISBN NUMBER 1-886104-03-4

Originally printed, 1999
First reprint edition, 2005

The Florida Historical Society Press
E-mail: wynne@flahistory.net

For my parents, who taught me there is a time to make war and a time to beat swords into plowshares.

Eliot Kleinberg
Casa Floridiana
Boca Raton, Fla.
January 1999

4/09

Table of Contents

"It was my first trip to Florida. I didn't like the experience. When I finally thought of my pals, they were in my prayers. I was a nervous wreck. The Germans? I figure it was war. It was their duty."

Frank Leonard Terry, the only survivor of thirty-six sailors aboard the *W. D. Anderson*, sunk about twelve miles north of Jupiter on February 22, 1942.

Introduction

With World War II starting with the invasion of Poland in 1939 and ending in the summer of 1945, the world was entering into a six-year 50th anniversary "window" in 1989. America's newspapers would be diving enthusiastically into a wild binge of coverage; the Palm Beach *Post*, my editors agreed, should be among them.

For the *Post*, newspaper of record for three counties from Boca Raton to Fort Pierce and out to Lake Okeechobee, marking the anniversary would be especially important. South Florida is heavy with retirees. The majority of our readers were there. And with seemingly everyone over the age of sixty-five in America now living in Florida, the state hosts one of the nation's largest contingents of World War II veterans.

While other newspapers might focus on far off battles or about veterans who moved to Florida recently but had left homes in New Jersey or Chicago to fight the Big War, I wanted to write about what had happened right here in Florida. Considering that the average Floridian has been here about ten minutes, anything I told our readers wouldn't be old news. It would be news.

Along the way, I learned that our fathers and grandfathers—and their female counterparts, more often than not unrecognized—were common people who committed acts of uncommon valor. Those of us who have never been asked to make that sacrifice can never know. We owe them our lives.

CHAPTER 1

Three Florida Boys at Pearl

An overcoat. A faded watch and a rusting key chain. A photograph from a carnival booth. Mementos, souvenirs, musty remnants of snuffed lives.

Red Hollis was a former Palm Beach cop who had braved a hurricane to help tell the world of the night 2,000 died.

Claude Edward Rich was a poor kid who saw the Navy as a way out of the Depression.

Eugene Lish played a mean clarinet for the Fort Pierce High School band. Bad feet put him on the wrong ship in the wrong harbor on the wrong Sunday.

The three died half a world from home on a day that, like no other in American history, still lives in infamy. Like other seminal events in our nation's history—Bunker Hill, Appomattox, Dallas—the Japanese attack that drew the United States into World War II is known simply by the place it happened. Lish now lies among the fallen at Arlington National Cemetery. The other two may have died in the same room and remain entombed there, inside a sunken ship called the *Arizona*, at a place called Pearl Harbor.

Survivors provide emotional testimony. But the dead cannot speak, and time has reduced them to names on a wall or faces in faded clippings. This is the story of common men caught up in a unique event; men from different paths whose lives developed in parallel, then collided on December 7, 1941.

The Promise of Youth—Ralph Hollis

"Red" Hollis' hair was the color of the clay in his native Georgia. The strapping teen from the hamlet of Godfrey, about 40 miles east of Atlanta, was valedictorian of 13 graduating seniors in 1923. Among his classmates was his third cousin, Hermione Campbell. Ralph Hollis wanted to attend Georgia Tech, but his parents had lost their cotton farm to boll weevils and the family was destitute. He hoped to attend the Naval Academy in Annapolis, but the man with the red hair was found to be colorblind. So in the fall, the 17-year-old signed on as an apprentice seaman in the Navy. Because he was too young, his father had to sign the induction papers. A scratched photograph shows a young, determined Ralph in full dress in front of an ornate curtain. Another shows him with sailor buddies at San Francisco's Golden Gate Park in April 1925, right before he left with the U.S. battle fleet on a five-month Pacific crossing to Hawaii, the place where he would die, and Australia. Sixteen years later, many of those same ships would lie quietly at Pearl Harbor as Japanese pilots centered them in their sites. During the crossing, on July 6, 1925, aboard the fueling ship *Kanawha*, Ralph became a "trusty shellback" when he crossed the equator near the Kiribati Islands, about 1,600 miles southwest of Hawaii.

Family was a priority for Ralph, and he sent part of his meager pay to send one of his six sisters to college. It was in the Navy that Ralph first developed the radio bug. When he got an honorable discharge March 22, 1926, he bought a motorcycle and traveled the west. When he returned, he was lured to South Florida. He drove his motorcycle to Palm Beach, where his brother was working, and got a job with the town's fire department. Ralph lived at the firehouse and set up his amateur radio equipment there.

His skills would later help him tell the world of America's third-deadliest natural disaster: the 1928 hurricane that overflowed Lake Okeechobee and killed 2,000 to 3,000 people. Just after midnight on Saturday, September 15, Ralph and his friend, police officer Forrest Dana, set up equipment and backup batteries on the second floor of the police station. By Sunday night, the winds had downed his aerial and partially flooded the room. About 6:30 a.m. Monday, as the storm moved inland toward the big lake, Ralph and Dana were the first to tell the world of the storm's fury.

"QST! QST! QST! This if 4AFC at Palm Beach, Florida. Urgent! Urgent! Urgent!" The report was brief and grim. Hundreds were dead, thousands of buildings demolished. Assistance was desperately needed. Dana and Ralph transmitted for 70 hours from the Palm Beach police station. Before the men finished at 3 a.m. Thursday, they had transmitted 10,000 words of news copy, 170 personal messages, 16 Red Cross messages to the agency's national headquarters, and 17 public messages, including an official appeal for troops.

"I have certainly been one busy fellow in the past eight days," he wrote his mother in Georgia.

Palm Beach Mayor Barclay Warburton later offered the gratitude of his constituents for the men's work. The Associated Press gave them engraved wristwatches.

On New Year's Day 1929, Ralph married Hermione Campbell, who had graduated Jackson Memorial Hospital's School of Nursing in Miami two years earlier. She moved in with him at 1707 Georgia Avenue in West Palm Beach. The marriage was a secret for four months. Before the Hollises' first anniversary, the country would be plunged into the Depression.

In the early 1930s, a widow gave a large donation to Palm Beach police to set up a radio system. Ralph was transferred from fire to police to develop it. He soon rose to lieutenant. Ralph wanted to start his own business in the fledgling radio industry. It was his single addiction. His equipment filled a wall at his home; it was more sophisticated than the regular radios that still only a few people owned. It pulled in stations near and far.

Despite his busy career, Ralph remained close to the Navy. On November 21, 1934, he enlisted in the Naval Reserve as an ensign. He was executive officer of the local reserve unit. When war began to rage in Europe, America girded for involvement. On May 6, 1941, Ralph was called to active duty. The Navy wanted to send him to Annapolis for a post-graduate course in communications. Because he had a wife and two children, the 34-year-old could have turned down the Navy. But he told his family, "If I have something my country needs, I think I owe it to my country to serve." The Navy told him war was very unlikely, and in any event, he wouldn't be near it. Ralph left his home at 808 Avon Road in West Palm Beach and headed to Annapolis. He finished August 16, 1941, and arrived at Pearl Harbor on September 18. He was commisioned a lieutenant and assigned as a communications watch officer, handling coding and intra-ship communications, aboard the *Arizona*.

Already aboard was Claude Rich.

Claude Edward Rich

The Palm Beach *Post* "Letters to Santa Claus" column of December 22, 1930, featured this plea: 'Dear Santa: I am a little boy eight years old. My father has no work so I hope you won't forget me. I have a brother and sister older than I am and I hope you won't forget them either this year. Claude Edward Rich, West Palm Beach."

When the boy became a man, he turned to the military as a way out of poverty. Claude was the only one of the three men who was a native of Palm Beach County. He was born February 4, 1922, in Riviera Beach, then called simply Riviera. His father, a commercial fisherman, had a tough time making ends meet for the family at 623 46th Street. The family had moved to South Florida from Oak Hill, near Daytona Beach.

Among Claude's buddies was Lester Covar, later a West Palm Beach police officer. The two lived a few blocks apart and would walk the half-dozen blocks to Northboro School. Claude and his buddy would ride their bikes to Bethesda Park—now Curry Park—where young people hung out. They would row johnboats out to the middle of the Intracoastal Waterway and drop hand lines. The bluefish would practically jump into the boat.

Claude was not a top student. He was two years older than the other 20 or so children in his class and may have repeated some years. But he was strong, and at 6-foot-2, was able to play softball and play end on Northboro's football team. One classmate was Elizabeth Albertson. He may have wanted to date her. But her father considered him beneath her.

Friends and relatives describe Claude as timid and gentle, not a fighter. But he had grown up rough in the tough blue collar neighborhood, and he would stick up for neighborhood kids when bullies picked on them. In the Depression, it was no shame to leave school early to start producing income for the family. Claude and Lester Covar landed jobs at Palm Beach Linen Service, now National Linen Service. Claude and Lester made deliveries and pickups at hotels, restaurants and barbershops from Delray Beach to Vero Beach. The work was hard, but there was always someone eager to take their place. They worked seven days a week for about $1 a day—a small sum but in a time when some places rented for $15 a month. Even at that, Claude lived at home to save money. As grueling as his work was, he still found time to help construct additions to Northwood Baptist Church's original building. And he took some radio lessons—from Ralph Hollis.

In 1940, Claude's father signed papers for him to enter the Navy. His mother pleaded that he remain in school. But his father said, "If that's what he wants..." It was not for any sense of patriotic duty or the desire to fight. Claude did it for the money, and he hoped his interest in radios would help him advance. Never did anyone consider the possibility he would come into harm's way. He boarded a bus for the nearest enlistment point—Macon, Ga. He reported for duty at Norfolk, Va., on September 22, 1940. He was 18. After a transfer to San Diego, another transfer took him to Pearl Harbor. Aboard his ship, he met Hollis, his old radio teacher. Claude was Seaman First Class, specializing in communications. His ship was the *Arizona*.

Eugene Victor Lish

Gene Lish was good enough on clarinet to get A's and a spot on the Fort Pierce High School band all four years. Gene was born September 20, 1920 in the central Florida town of Davenport. His father, a recipient of the Croix de Guerre—France's war cross—in World War I, had moved from *West Virginia* to try the booming citrus industry. When that venture stalled, he used his railroad experience to get a job as an engineer with the Florida East Coast railroad. FEC had a "round house"—a place where locomotives rotated on a giant hub as cars were attached—in Fort Pierce, then a cow and citrus town of about 5,000. The facility was the largest between St. Augustine and Miami. Wilbur Wordan Lish moved his family to 805 Delaware Avenue in Fort Pierce, now a law office. He spent the then-large sum of $7,000 to have the house built. It was a walk of about a block to Fort Pierce School, now an elementary school.

Gene shined only in band. He earned B's and D's in Latin and B's and C's in history and struggled even harder with algebra and English. He loved to travel and he saw the country on his father's railroad pass. He took his first airplane ride in 1934. He got chicken pox as a youngster and broke his rib when he was ten. A year later, on March 9, 1931, he took his first music lesson—in violin. His first recital was two years later, at the Sunrise Theater, where he would also see cowboy star Tom Mix. He later gravitated toward the clarinet. In the school's band, he was second clarinetist. Fellow band member Ann Nobles Miller recalls the lanky Gene as an intelligent, funny guy. The band held concerts and played at ball games. It also marched in Fourth of July parades that featured veterans of World War I. Gene watched soldiers without eyes, arms, or legs. It left him shaken but determined.

"I don't know much about this Hitler guy but I know war's coming and I want to be involved," he said. "I have yet to meet a one-legged sailor," he told his young brother Earl. "If I go into the service, I will go in the Navy. Either you come back in one piece or you don't come back."

First Gene wanted to improve his grades. So he voluntarily repeated his senior year, graduating in 1939. Then Gene boarded a train for Washington with his father. The young man wanted to attend the U.S. Navy Music School, serve his country and sock away money to attend Oberlin College in Ohio. He passed the Navy physical. On the way out, his father said he was surprised doctors hadn't noted his bad feet. "What bad feet?" the startled doctor said. Wilbur Lish's heart jumped to his throat. He sadly shook his head. "I shouldn't have said anything." Gene dutifully removed his shoes. Sure enough, the pinky toe on both feet curled around on top of its neighbor. Correcting the problem was a simple operation that could be performed in an office visit and later was. But the delay meant Gene couldn't enter the school until the first training session of 1940. Had he been able to attend the Fall 1939 session, Gene would have been assigned to the *North Carolina*, which saw little action until late 1942. Later in the war, its band was sent permanently to play at a naval base stateside. That his casual comment about his son's feet indirectly led to Gene's death at

Pearl Harbor weighed heavily on Wilbur Lish for the rest of his life.

Gene graduated the Navy Music School on April 30, 1941, as a Musician Second Class. On his last visit home, he showed off his military band uniform to his old friends in the high school band. But his mother had a premonition.

"I'll never see him alive again," she told Claude's brother Earl.

"Mom, whaddya mean? We're not at war," the youngster said.

Gene was assigned the *West Virginia*, namesake of his father's home state. Its base: Pearl Harbor. It was, his brother says, the *wrong* ship, the *wrong* harbor, and the *wrong* Sunday.

Pearl Harbor

Before heading out to Pearl Harbor, Red Hollis had set up his wife, Hermione, and two daughters — Louise, then 12, and Mary Ann, 18 months — in Long Beach, Calif. Hermione and the girls made plans to visit Ralph in Hawaii on New Year's Day 1942. He sent a letter December 1 to his mother in Georgia. In it, he said, "Within a week we will be at war with Japan." He did not elaborate. The letter arrived after his death.

Claude Rich's time on the *Arizona* was not without its down side. Claude once went AWOL for 19 hours; he had to face a "deck court martial" — a one-man tribunal for serious but not grievous infractions. He was confined for five days and had to pay what was then a hefty fine of $9. He wrote his family that he wanted a transfer to the East Coast. He wrote his brother, stationed in the Navy in Rhode Island, that he planned to visit. In letters to his buddy, Lester Covar, he never mentioned the threat of war. His major concern was his homesickness. He wrote Covar in November 1941 that he was getting leave December 14 and planned to be home for Christmas. It was the last word any of Claude Rich's friends or relatives ever got from him.

Gene Lish was good about writing home to Fort Pierce. A July 30, 1941, note from "At Sea," contained the usual complaints. There were four showers for 600 men, he spent half his time folding and unfolding things, and lockers were so small "that even the roaches get in each others' way." Other letters said he was putting away a $50 government bond each month for college and was up to $600. When he was promoted to Musician First Class, Gene said, "I passed out the cigars!" He got a raise and the key to the petty officers' washroom ("there is always hot water") along with a large locker and "the best cot space in the band." And he would start directing the marches that took place every morning at eight o'clock on the quarterdeck.

Letters gave insight to mundane things. A dentist filled his tooth. His watch had a broken jewel that he fixed for $6.50. He went to boxing matches and a battle of the bands and spent a day at Waikiki Beach. He played bingo and won a linen handkerchief and a bottle of aftershave. He saw the films *Here Comes Mr. Jordan* and *Citizen Kane* aboard ship. He hung out with the band from the *Arizona*. But Gene was homesick as well, "If this place didn't look so much like Fla., I'd probably be going nuts as the other fellow officers are."

He asked what the family wanted for Christmas.

"Please let me know and maybe I can get it before the rush. Above all, don't ask for a Hawaiian souvenir. They are just like the ones at home only not so good. The hula skirts, etc. sold out here are made in Chicago."

But there were also hints those in Hawaii knew who their enemy would be if war ever broke out.

"We're sinking the Japanese Navy right and left," Gene joked in one letter. He also denied a German news report that his ship, the *West Virginia*, and most of the fleet had left for Japan.

"Because of all the Navy ships being torpedoed in the Atlantic we have been given all kinds of watches during the day," he wrote. "They have been giving us all kinds of drills and general quarters in case something happens out here."

A November 23 letter says, "A few minutes ago, we secured from Condition II watches"—the one stood at all times during wartime. Earplugs sent by his brother did little to suppress the booming of the ship's giant guns during drills. On December 1, Gene sent a Christmas card ("Mele Kalikimaka from Hawaii") to be forwarded to his Aunt Rosie, whose address he didn't have, "but I want her to know I'm thinking of her." Four days later, the *WeeVee* returned from maneuvers at sea.

The next day, Saturday, December 6, Gene spent the afternoon drinking beer with a friend. They attended a battle of the bands won by the one from the *Arizona*. Within 24 hours, everyone in that group would be dead. Gene had a few more beers. Back home, in Fort Pierce, 5-1/2 hours ahead of Hawaii time, his family was already asleep. Gene Lish returned to the *West Virginia* for the last night of his life.

December 7, 1941

December 7, 1941, was cool and rainy in South Florida.

Nine people had been hurt the night before in a two-car accident in Loxahatchee. The Delray Beach Recreation Club and the Gulf Stream Bath and Tennis Club were opening for the season. A fur coat sold for $49.95 at the

Mather Co. in West Palm Beach. A community sing-along was scheduled for 3 p.m. at the band shell in Stuart. In Hobe Sound, a new diner opened to serve the thousands of soldiers training at nearby Camp Murphy, now Jonathan Dickinson State Park. The diner is now the Harry and the Natives bar and restaurant. The Sunday morning paper carried an ominous front page story: "President Roosevelt has dispatched a personal message to Emperor Hirohito of Japan in the midst of darkening war clouds in the Far East."

Soon it was mid-afternoon in West Palm Beach; 7:55 a.m. in Pearl Harbor.

While most band members on the *West Virginia* were stretcher bearers during battle stations, three, including Gene Lish, were "talkers." It was their job to don headsets and give orders throughout the ship. If word came of wounded, they were to pass that on to doctors and direct the stretchers.

"We're below the water line, so there's not much chance of being hit, but if the ship goes down, I'll probably go with it," he had written.

Gene and fellow band member Donie Calderone had pulled guard shifts that Sunday morning. They were drinking coffee twenty feet from their bunks, one deck down, when they heard an airplane pass overhead and felt the ship shake.

"What the hell's going on?" Calderone exclaimed.

Many of the ships in the harbor were undergoing routine repair and maintenance, and Calderone's first reaction was, "Some SOB probably hit us with a tug." Then the second torpedo hit. Dining tables stored overhead crashed to the floor. Seconds later came the announcement: "General quarters. This is no drill. We are being attacked." Gene and Calderone scrambled to their battle stations. Gene went below to the third deck, next to the brig, near the center of the ship.

The *West Virginia* was tied to the *Tennessee*, dead center in the line of attack. It took seven torpedoes, which broke open fuel compartments. Fumes from the low-grade crude oil filled the lower decks. Gene was among those overpowered. Two people tried to pull his limp body up a ladder and through a porthole to the next deck. But they too were overcome and had to abandon him. With the ship partially sunk and at a list, two stretcher bearers carrying Gene slipped on the oil-slick deck and slid into the water with him. No one knows if he drowned then or was already dead.

One-hundred and six men died on the *West Virginia* – only one from the band. Newspaper clippings declared Gene the first Floridian killed in a war too new to have a name. The *West Virginia* was the first ship attacked,

8

at 7:56 a.m., so if Gene was killed immediately, he was just minutes ahead of Ralph Hollis and Claude Rich.

Little is known of the fates of Ralph and Claude. Because there had been time to call battle stations, and because the two were radio specialists, both were probably in the radio room, three decks below. The *Arizona* took four direct hits from 1,760-pound converted battleship shells dropped by the Japanese pilots. The deadliest one struck just about 8:05 a.m. It crashed through the deck beside the No. 2 turret, near the front of the ship, and into a fuel tank next to the forward powder magazine. Seconds later 1.7 million pounds of gunpowder ignited. Flames shot 500 feet in the air and the foremast—directly above the radio room—tilted sharply as the ship lifted up, broke apart and sank almost immediately to the bottom of the shallow harbor. One serviceman blown from the deck of a nearby ship by the force of the blast said the *Arizona* "blew up like a million Fourth of Julys."

It is believed about 1,000 of the 1,103 deaths on the *Arizona*—half of the death toll at Pearl Harbor—occurred at that moment. Men on deck were seen staggering a few steps, their clothes blown from their bodies, and falling dead. Others were blown to bits. The radio room was about 50 feet from the center of the blast. Relatives and friends believe Ralph Hollis—and Claude Rich if he was there as well—were killed instantly, perhaps among those vaporized by the explosion. As the planes bearing red suns on their wings turned for home, they left behind 18 of the 92 ships in port sunk or heavily damaged, and 188 airplanes destroyed. And 2,403 military personnel and civilians were dead—including Ralph Hollis, Claude Rich, and Gene Lish.

Next of Kin

It was radio, which Ralph Hollis loved, that brought his family first word of the attack. It was around lunchtime in Long Beach. Young Louise Hollis clung to the radio and felt her mother's desperation. It grew intense when the announcer said the *Arizona* had been hit. For some reason, the Navy didn't have Hermione Hollis' number in California. Officials called Georgia about 1 a.m. A neighbor who had a phone got Ralph's father, who learned he was missing in action. He called Hermione in California. The December 10 Palm Beach *Post* said only that Ralph was stationed at Pearl Harbor and the last word from him had been a November 27 Christmas card to his sister in West Palm Beach that had arrived December 9.

A telegram came to Long Beach on Monday, December 15:

"If remains are recovered they will be interred temporarily in the locality where death occurred and you will be notified accordingly," said the wire, signed by Rear Admiral Chester W. Nimitz, then chief of the bureau of navigation. A brother-in-law of Hermione's flew to California to drive Hermione and the devastated family back to West Palm Beach in Ralph's car in time for Christmas. Ralph was not immediately declared dead, and that prompted a bureaucratic nightmare for his widow. The Navy stopped paying her. She couldn't secure her legal or financial affairs and had to live off her savings. Relatives say she was strong for the children.

December 7, 1941, was the longest day ever for Claude's Rich's brother. Jesse Rich, also in the Navy, was on a 10-day leave from Rhode Island. He and his family were sitting around the house in the afternoon. They always kept the radio on. At word of the attack, Jesse walked outside, shaken, and stood there a long while. The announcers were saying several ships had already been sunk. Damage reports grew more intense. Jesse figured it looked grim for his brother. Claude's mother cried all day but said little. His father feared the worst. About a dozen friends came to the house to offer support. The telegram came ten days later, confirming that Claude was missing in action. With no body, the wounds stayed open. Jesse walked off. He later turned himself in at Miami to face punishment for being ten days overdue to return to base. The Navy went easy on him. They considered the circumstances.

Lester Covar didn't know his friend was dead until a letter he had sent was returned, stamped "deceased."

At Northwood Baptist Church, on the banner at the north end of the sanctuary honoring the men in the service, a star went up.

Up the road in Fort Pierce, Earl Lish, 15, was playing football with friends. His mother telephoned.

"Come home," she said. "Pearl Harbor's been attacked."

He said, "Where's Pearl Harbor?"

"That's where your brother is."

Earl Lish raced the 10 blocks home on his bicycle. The next 11 days were a hell of uncertainty. On the evening of December 8, Gene's mother had awoken from a dream. She had seen her son with rays of light emanating behind him. She knew then he was dead. On December 18, Gene's mother called the high school to send Earl home; official word had come of Gene's death. Ten minutes later, the flag was lowered to half-staff. At a memorial service, a call to buy defense bonds to honor Gene's memory caused a stampede. St. Andrew's Church listed 39 names for men in the service, marked with blue stars, and one gold star for Gene Lish.

Aftermath

10

The bodies of Ralph Hollis and Claude Edward Rich were never recovered. They are presumed to be among the 650 to 900 men entombed in the *Arizona*, now a national cemetery. Ralph Hollis received the Purple Heart, American Defense service medal, Asiatic Pacific Area campaign medal and World War II Victory medal. The West Palm Beach City Commission passed a resolution December 23, 1941, honoring Ralph, who "Almighty God, in His Infinite Wisdom, has seen fit to call into a better world."

In February 1991, Palm Beach photographer Frank Turgeon displayed an exhibition of color photographs in the courtyard of the Paramount Theater building in Palm Beach. The premier picture was that of Ralph Hollis.

In 1943, Palm Beach County raised war bonds to pay for the building of the *Hollis*, a 2,130-ton, 306-foot escort ship. The ship was in Tokyo Harbor, near the *Missouri*, when the Japanese surrendered in 1945. On March 7, 1954, in front of 3,000 people at the Port of Palm Beach, Hermione Hollis presented a plaque to hang on the *Hollis* in its first visit to its unofficial homeport.

Hermione Hollis died in 1985 in West Palm Beach. Louise Hollis lives near New Orleans, her sister in east Texas. The *Hollis* was later mothballed.

Claude Rich was awarded the Purple Heart, American Defense service medal and World War II Victory medal. His parents also received a citation from President Roosevelt, which read "He stands in the unbroken line of patriots who have dared to die that freedom might live and increase its blessings. Freedom lives and through it, he lives in a way that humbles the undertaking of most men."

Claude's friend Elizabeth Albertson, who as a teenager was forbidden to date Claude because her family thought him beneath her, keeps a picture in her *Bible*. It is Claude's name on the wall of the *Arizona* memorial. Lester Covar's anger over the attack and his friend's death prompted him to go to the U.S. Post Office downtown, where he stood in a long line of other angry people wanting to enlist. But the military wouldn't take him, citing his wife and child. Over the years, Lester Covar watched, not with envy but with sadness, as Ralph Hollis got all the attention. In 1961, on the twentieth anniversary of the attack, he called the Palm Beach *Post* to urge a story on the other local martyr of Pearl Harbor. In 1990, for his fiftieth wedding anniversary, Lester Covar's children offered him a trip. The retired police officer's options were to see his ancestral home in Switzerland or his buddy's name. He chose Hawaii. As he stood above the wreck of the *Arizona*, it occurred to him that his friend lay somewhere beneath his feet. Covar died in October 1999.

Claude Rich's father never really held his head up again. He always remembered it was he who had signed the papers for Claude to join up. Claude's father was dead within two years. His mother died in 1959. His brother, Jesse Bill Rich, lives in Nevada.

Gene Lish got the Purple Heart, American Defense Service medal, World War II Victory medal, Asiatic-Pacific Campaign Medal and Good Conduct Medal. Philip Nourse, later a circuit court judge in Fort Pierce, was at his fraternity house at the University of Florida when he learned his friend was dead. He pulled from his wallet a $2 bill—the currency the Navy used for pay—that he had bought from Gene. Nourse would carry the bill for more than twenty years. Nourse was so offended by the Japanese attack and angry about his friend's death that two weeks later he enlisted.

Gene's body was recovered and joined others in a mass grave. An acquaintance positively identified him and his coffin was marked with his name. Fellow band member Howard Hare cleaned out the large locker Gene had been so proud to obtain. His clothes and instruments were found burned. Inside a charred case, Hare found Gene's glasses and sent them to Gene's mother in Fort Pierce. Donie Calderone went to a Catholic church and lit a candle for his dead pal.

For eight years the Lishes could not close the book on Gene. There was no body, no coffin, no funeral. In 1949, the military offered relatives a choice to have their loved ones removed from the mass burial site and buried at Arlington National Cemetery in Virginia. The Lishes could not bear the stress of the funeral. Former neighbors living in Washington attended for them. Florida Representative George Smathers and Senator Spessard Holland sent representatives. It was a warm sunny day. A Navy band played *Nearer My God to Thee*, the tune played by the band on the sinking *Titanic*. Earl Lish has a photograph of his young granddaughter kneeling at Gene Lish's tombstone at Arlington, among the rows that seem to stretch to the horizon.

On August 13, 1944, Fort Pierce Post 3064 of the Veterans of Foreign Wars was named for Eugene Lish. The *West Virginia* was repaired. It was the first ship from the Pearl Harbor attack to anchor in Tokyo Bay during the Japanese surrender.

Gene's father continued as an engineer, retiring in 1958 with fifty-one years of railroad service, thirty-eight for Florida East Coast Railroad. Newspapers covered his "last ride." He died in 1972. Earl Lish is now an engineer for Martin Marietta in Orlando.

Gene's face smiles out from grade school pictures in his brother's scrapbooks. There are pictures of Gene and Earl with their parents, the two as infants, Gene as "The Brownie Dunce Josh" in a grade school play, Gene bumming at the beach with friends and in his band uniform with his clarinet. There's a shot taken at the school that reveals a very-forbidden cigarette in his right hand. Then there are pictures of Gene in his Navy uniform and at the music school in Washington. And there is the picture from January 1941 of Gene in his Navy music school uniform, crouching, a big grin on his face. It is the picture that hangs at the VFW post named for him. Above the photograph is the flag that draped Gene's coffin just before it was lowered into its grave at Arlington; the flag that flew over the St. Lucie County Courthouse on August 24, 1949.

Earl Lish, who died in July 1992, kept two items found on his brother's body. One is a key chain, with three keys, a pocketknife and three charms—medals from Gene's days at Fort Pierce High. There's his graduation charm from 1939, along with a medal indicating his membership in the band. The third item is a "solo award" from a band competition in 1939 in West Palm Beach. The other is Gene's watch. The hands have long since fallen off, but Earl Lish would point to a shadow on the glass, a line pointing to the "2." He says the watch was found with Gene, frozen at 8:10 a.m.—fifteen minutes after the Japanese attacked Pearl Harbor.

For years, Lester Covar kept mementos of his friend Claude Rich. A few years back, when he moved to a trailer in Melbourne, he finally had to throw them out. One was a photograph. A midway would come once a year to a field where West Palm Beach City Hall now stands, and a photo booth at the carnival captured two happy teenagers who thought they could live forever.

Among the souvenirs of Ralph Hollis' life, one moves his daughter the most. It is an inventory, dated February 19, 1942, of all the personal effects of her father that were salvaged from the *Arizona*:

"1 officers rain coat."

Pearl Harbor Attack Facts

U.S. Losses:
2,403 killed
1,175 wounded
8 battleships sunk or severely damaged
3 cruisers sunk
3 destroyers sunk
2 auxiliary ships sunk
1 minelayer sunk
1 target battleship sunk
188 aircraft lost

The *USS Arizona*
Launched in 1915, a *Pennsylvania* class battleship; modernized with radar in 1940
Displacement: 33,100 tons
Armed with 12 14-inch guns
1,103 crewmembers killed in Pearl Harbor attack
Memorial built atop wreck attracts 4,500 visitors a day

The *USS West Virginia*:
Launched in 1921, third ship of the *Colorado* class
Displacement: 32,600 tons
Armed with eight 16-inch guns
Repaired after Pearl Harbor; damaged by kamikaze April 1945

Japanese Losses
64 men dead or missing
1 prisoner of war
29 planes lost
1 submarine lost
5 midget subs lost

Ralph `Red' Hollis:
Born: September 10, 1906, Godfrey, Georgia
Education: High school class of 1923, valedictorian
Married: January 1, 1929 to Hermione Campbell
Service Record: Enlisted in the Navy as apprentice seaman, fall 1923; discharged, March 1926. Joined Naval Reserve November 1934. Called to

active duty May 1941. Reported aboard battleship *Arizona* September 18, 1941. Posthumously received Purple Heart, the American Defense service medal, the Asiatic Pacific Area campaign medal and World War II Victory medal.

`Within a week we will be at war with Japan." — Ralph Hollis in a letter to his mother dated December 1, 1941*

Claude Rich:
Born: February 4, 1922, Riviera Beach
Education: Left school early to work during the Depression.
Service Record: Enlisted in the Navy in September 1940. Transferred to San Diego, then assigned to the battleship *Arizona*. Posthumously received the Purple Heart, the American Defense service medal and the World War II Victory medal.

"He stands in the unbroken line of patriots who have dared to die that freedom might live and increase its blessings." — President Franklin Roosevelt in a citation to Claude Rich's parents

Eugene Lish:
Born: September 12, 1920, Davenport, Iowa
Education: Fort Pierce High School, 1939
Service Record: Enlisted in the Navy in early 1940; Graduated Navy music school, April 1941; Assigned to the battleship *West Virginia*. Award the Purple Heart, the American Defense Service Medal, the World War II Victory Medal, the Asiatic-Pacific Campaign Medal and the Good Conduct Medal. Buried in Arlington National cemetery in 1949.

"If this place didn't look so much like Fla, I'd probably be going nuts as the other fellow officers are." — Eugene Lish in a letter home from Hawaii.

Ralph "Red" Hollis, a former Palm Beach policeman, died aboard the *Arizona*. (Photo courtesy of the Hollis Family)

Eugene Lish of Fort Pierce died on the *West Virginia*. (Photo courtesy of the Lish Family)

Claude Eugene Rich of West Palm Beach joined the Navy for a better life. He was killed on the battleship *Arizona*. (Photo courtesy of the Palm Beach *Post*)

FIRST LOCAL BORN BOY LOST IN WAR

CLAUD E. RICH

West Palm Beach's first native

CHAPTER 2

The War Offshore

If you were living on the resort area of Jupiter Island, along southern Florida's Treasure Coast, on February 21, 1942, you might have been partying at the local drinking hole, relaxing in your living room, or asleep in bed. All of a sudden, you would have felt the ground beneath you vibrate. You would have heard a boom in the distance, so powerful it rattled dishes and windows and even broke some. You might even have been knocked out of bed. Far off at sea, you might have seen a dull white glow. A short time later, you might see two lifeboats pull up to the beach behind your house. Several men would stagger off, coated in oil. They would be the crew of the *Republic*.

You would then discover that living on America's coast had suddenly come with a price. America was at war, and the war had come literally to your back yard. If you lived in America's heartland, you knew the war all too well; you sent your sons and husbands, and some didn't come back. But you never really felt personal fear. The war was in strange lands far across the sea. But if you lived on the coast of Florida or across coastal America, from Maine to South Texas, you could see the war glowing on the horizon. You could see its smoke billowing and feel its heat. You could encounter its dead tangled in seaweed on the beach. And you lived with a special fear reserved for civilians in war's way. You went to bed every night wondering if a shell would crash down on you while you slept. After all, just offshore just a few feet below the pleasure boaters and commercial fishermen the metal sharks lay in wait.

In those first few weeks after Pearl Harbor pulled America headlong into a two-front war, the *untersee* boots of Adolf Hitler's navy worked with virtual impunity. Off Florida alone, they sank twenty-four ships. Sixteen went down in a 150-mile stretch of Florida coastline from Cape Canaveral to Boca Raton between February and May 1942. With little or no resistance, the U-boats could leisurely stalk the lumbering tankers and freighters working their way up the coast. Their periscope sights would spot their prey silhouetted in the lights of the oceanfront hotels that drew tourists in droves to Florida.

17

The commanders were under strict orders to sink ships, nothing more. Hitler's plans at that point didn't include massacring civilians in American cities. But South Floridians didn't know that. They painted their headlights black, took part in blackouts and drills, patrolled beaches on foot or on horseback. Jumpy authorities rounded up virtually anyone with a German-sounding accent or Asian features. Rumors spread like fire on an oil slick. And some of the very features that attracted tourists to Florida made it the logical place for soldiers as well.

The state, a strategic asset for its geography and climate, became an armed camp. Its hotels turned into barracks. Hospitals, bases and airfields sprang up, increasing from eight in 1940 to one hundred and seventy-two in 1943. The influx of soldiers led to the boom that changed Florida's population from about two million in 1940 to nearly three million a decade later. The sleepy southern locale became one of the nation's most important and fastest-growing states.

"Suddenly we found ourselves one of the most important territories for one of the most important wars of all times," Miami history professor Paul George said.

Florida would never be the same.

"Hanging Like A Pall"

"Don't strike matches or show a light in any way. Don't light a cigarette...take refuge in a nearby building and stay there until the all-clear signal."

Authorities weren't messing around when they conducted a practice blackout January 11, 1942, that threw into darkness a 300-mile stretch of South Florida coastline from Stuart to Key West. At 10:15 that night, city lights switched off in sweeping waves.

"It was an impressive and sobering sight," wrote one reporter as he stood on a rooftop and watched the twin tourist towns of West Palm Beach and Palm Beach enveloped in black, "to see these two large municipalities as dark as a pocket when the huge observation plane soared over the resorts, its throbbing motors breaking the stillness, which seemed to hang like a pall over everything."

The war footing touched everyone. Beachfront hotels and restaurants, worried about business, initially resisted orders for coastal cities to dim lights so ships wouldn't be backlit. It was not until April 11, 1942, that Governor Spessard Holland ordered a dimming of lights facing the sea. Streetlights were hooded to cast only a small circle of light directly down. Ten donated station wagons were fitted with blankets as emergency standby ambulances.

"The fear was tremendously real along the coast," said Paul George, former president of the Florida Historical Society. "It was a visible fear. You could see the plumes of black smoke off the coast. You felt a fear that few other parts of the United States felt. You saw the damage first hand of the Nazi war machine."

"We witnessed several encounters offshore — flares, rockets, gunfire," recalled Joy S. Kissam of North Palm Beach. "Since security was tight, we never knew exactly what we were seeing."

"We had a manual telephone switchboard in Lake Worth, the kind where the operator said, 'Number please. Thank you,'" recalled Florence B. Schnopp of Lake Worth. About 4 o'clock one morning a man in the luxurious oceanfront community of Manalapan, south of Palm Beach, called the switchboard, she recalled. "He said, 'Operator, there's a ship on fire,'" she said. "He called his friends in Palm Beach and they brought their big coffee urns and blankets for the boys, who had to swim through burning oil to get to shore..."

Kathleen R. Pacetti of West Palm Beach and a friend were spotters for the Army's Aircraft Warning Service. They spent every Saturday from 10 a.m. to noon in a room on the roof of a downtown building.

"We were cautioned not to report bobbing coconuts — there were lots of them — or pelicans — lots of them too — in our excitement," Pacetti said.

Round Up the Usual Suspects

Paranoia led authorities to detain people on the slightest suspicion of subterfuge. In the first days following the attack on Pearl Harbor, FBI agents and local police were under strict orders to pick up any Japanese. "Loafers" unknown to police were to be run off and any aliens held for questioning. The FBI searched a Japanese-owned import-export shop on Palm Beach's ritzy Worth Avenue and posted an armed sailor out front who answered no questions from nosy reporters. Newspaper accounts said the shop "appeared empty except for some glass showcases, and the search was believed to be in line with the national investigation of everything Japanese." FBI agents picked up I.H. Okamato of the Nippon Dry Goods Company, Los Angeles, after a Chinese cook at his hotel advised police.

The former Countess Erica von Haacke, of the Silesia region of Germany, was "taken into custody" in Palm Beach while wintering from New Jersey with her family. A newspaper story appeared to identify the countess as one of two unnamed people arrested in South Florida. The story said the FBI detained the two — one Italian, one German, both members of their homeland's nobility and both prominent in the social circles of South Florida's winter residents—in a nationwide sweep. The story said agents found shortwave radios, camera equipment and cameras in the detainees' homes, one in Palm Beach and one in Miami. And the FBI arrested Baron Fritz von Opel—yachtsman, scion of the Opel carmaker family, and inventor of the rocket-propelled car—on February 26, 1942, at his Palm Beach residence along with his wife and two Hungarians. Authorities labeled them "potential dangerous aliens."

By late February 1942, news reports showed, FBI agents had made fifty-five raids in the West Palm Beach and Fort Lauderdale areas, arresting twenty-nine suspected enemy aliens and confiscating guns and cameras.

February 28, 1942 was the deadline for "enemy aliens" to register with the federal government; failure brought the threat of interment for the duration of the war. Unlike their West Coast counterparts, Japanese residents of Florida—the state's 1940 census lists only 217 statewide—were not subject to the mass relocation to government-run camps. But that did not protect them from FBI investigations or other restrictions meant to prevent espionage.

The government froze the assets of George Morikami, former member of the Yamato colony in Boca Raton. It ran his farm and lodged servicemen in his home. He had to get permission to travel outside the county. The government also confiscated land owned by the Yamato colony family of Hideo Kobayashi for the Boca Raton Army Air Field. To avoid the wartime regulations that would not permit them to cross a county line to conduct their landscaping business, the Kobayashis moved twenty miles south to Fort Lauderdale.

The Coast Watch

The Coast Guard set up observation towers every three miles, at places like the Lake Worth casino. Instructions were specific and grim. If an airplane was spotted, the watcher was to dash to the phone:

"When the central operator hears the words 'Army-Flash,' she immediately starts to put through a high priority, Government collect, long-distance call to the Army Filter Center..."

A polo grounds held barracks for about 280 U.S. Coast Guard beach watchers. The men, each armed with a .38-caliber pistol strapped to their waist and a rifle in their boot, rode horses shipped in from Fort Riley, Kansas. The horses initially rode up to sixteen miles a night before a leader devised a plan to ship the horses to strategic points to cut the riding to six miles. Teenagers who had never been in a saddle were drafted for their local knowledge and rode eight to ten hours a night. Where horses couldn't maneuver, thirty trained dogs took over.

"I have many memories of walking dogs on the beach with sand flies biting under my leggings and making it very uncomfortable to say the least," recalled Fran Wagner of Okeechobee, who was a Coast Guard spotter in Fort Pierce.

Motorists along the coast reported submarine sightings. Excited residents jammed the switchboards at Morrison Field, now Palm Beach International Airport in West Palm Beach; authorities forwarded sighting reports to Washington. By the time authority was given to scramble a plane, any U-boats were long gone. The paranoia was mostly unnecessary, although citizens could not have known that, Florida historian Dr. Michael Gannon said.

"Nowhere in German U-boat operations do you find the U-boat force shelling civilian targets to create terror or fear," Gannon said. "They lacked the weapons to do any substantial military damage, so what was the point? They were not given to that kind of behavior."

Authorities got a break in early 1942 when a big winter storm blocked Jupiter Inlet, about 25 miles north of West Palm Beach, for the duration of the war, enabling horseback and Jeep patrols to negotiate most of the coastline.

The nation's third Civil Air Patrol squadron formed at Morrison Field.

The "Coastal Picket Patrol" and the "Mosquito Fleet"—rag-tag flotillas of pleasure and charter boats—patrolled for subs and rescued survivors from torpedoed ships.

At "The Hill," the complex just west of downtown West Palm Beach that housed Palm Beach High School, Junior High and Elementary, stories of sinkings, attacks and Germans coming ashore flew through classrooms. Teachers would hush students, saying, "If you didn't see it, don't talk about it. The enemy might be listening."

Patrol dogs ran people off the beaches at night. And anyone crossing the bridges between West Palm Beach and Palm Beach encountered an armed sentry who shined his flashlight, demanded identification and sometimes searched cars. Just to cross the bridges, residents had to be fingerprinted and photographed for an ID card.

"Access to the beaches in the daytime was hardly interrupted during this time, so long as one wore the badge," recalled Persis Haas Newman, then a junior at Palm Beach High School and now living in Indiana. "Night access was out of the question," Newman said. "No more beach parties with the bonfire." Instead, the light came from ships burning at sea.

A Massacre

In the first half-year of war, the Germans sank 397 ships and killed some 5,000 people, about twice as many as died in Hawaii on December 7, 1941. University of Florida professor Michael Gannon, in the 1990 book *Operation Drumbeat*, called it "a six-months long massacre, compared with which the defeat at Pearl Harbor was but a rap on the knuckles." Gannon alleges monumental incompetence and delay by American authorities. He said they knew the subs' locations from British intelligence but weren't prepared to fight them and were too focused on the war in the Pacific. The German strategy was to interrupt the flow of supplies along the U.S. coast and to England, lay waste to the Allies' merchant fleet and strike a propaganda blow by letting Americans watch burning ships from their beaches.

"The Axis submarine campaign was well planned," a U.S. Navy report said at the time. "Nowhere else in the world could (Germany) find such a concentration of ships in such a small area." The Germans, smarting from losses in the Atlantic, saw an opportunity to prey on tankers plying the crowded and narrow shipping lanes off the Florida coast, where traffic ranked second in the United States and sixth in the world.

Reports said about one of every 12 ships sunk worldwide in 1942 went down in Florida waters. Northbound ships riding the Gulf Stream, the powerful current in the Atlantic Ocean that hugs South Florida's coast, and southbound ones squeezed between the stream and the coast were funneled into a narrow killing field. The Florida attacks killed hundreds of men and sent millions of dollars in cargo and oil to the bottom. Coast Guard and Navy ships and volunteers rescued about 500 seamen and saved some of the cargo. The "Gulf Sea Frontier" defensive force was responsible for 45,814 miles of serpentine coastline from Maine to the Texas-Mexico border, a distance nearly equal to two trips around the world. But it was ill-equipped to fight the roving bulldogs of the sea. Many ships had been given to the British. The Canadian Navy, expected to help, was in bad shape as well. And the U.S. Navy had focused on escorts across the Atlantic. As a result, defenders had six ships, four under repair, and 15 unarmed planes, 14 planes with machine guns and three ancient B-18 bombers that spent more time in the shop than in the air. Defenders say that, not ineptitude, gave the advantage to the Germans.

The brash U-boat commanders enjoyed the luxury of selecting their targets, holding fire on empty boats and waiting for those heavy with cargo and low in the water. They would watch for the slow moving, winking lights that betrayed their prey. Then they would flee pursuers as the officers of the sinking boats tossed confidential codes overboard and crewmembers scrambled for lifeboats.

"Sy's Men's Store did a big business dressing the survivors of some of those oil tankers that were blown out of the water," recalled Dora Digby of Palm Beach. "At the local night spots, they were usually celebrating the survivors—on the house, of course."

Emergency workers at Good Samaritan Hospital in West Palm Beach saw as many as fifty seamen in a night, some foreigners unable to describe injuries ranging from broken bones to oil burns. Many who could speak English were too busy screaming in agony. One night, a loud boom shook Carolyn Beaty Darr's water pitcher in a back room of the hospital, where Darr was a supervisor on the 11 p.m. to 7 a.m. shift. Two hours later, the injured started arriving.

"These men were all European, spoke no English and were so burned and swollen we could not even tell what they looked like," recalled Darr, now retired in Jupiter. On good nights, survivors came ashore. On bad nights, far less washed up.

The War Was Right There!

The first Florida victim of *Operation Drumbeat* was the 23-year-old, 8,200-ton *Pan Massachusetts*, hit in broad daylight by two torpedoes off Cape Canaveral on February 19. It had been heading north from Texas to New York with more than four million gallons of oil. The attacker—submarine U-128. Twenty of 38 crewmen died. Lifeboats and rafts were consumed by flame. A passing British tanker picked up survivors. The ship broke up and sank fifty miles north of Jupiter Lighthouse.

Two days later, at 11 p.m., the *Republic* was hit 3-1/2 miles northeast of the lighthouse by submarine U-504. The 22-year-old, 5,882-ton tanker, sailing empty south from New Jersey for Texas, had been recently fitted with guns but the attack was so sudden they were never used.

Stuart insurance agent Ralph Hartman recalled that night. It was his 18th birthday and a week away from his brother's 16th birthday, reason enough for the gang to drive the few miles up from Stuart to Jensen Beach to celebrate. As Hartman dropped a nickel in the jukebox, the pilings sunk into the Indian River began vibrating. The tremors moved up the floor of Seymour's Inn and right up Hartman's legs. There was a dull boom. The building shook and windows rattled. Ralph and his pals dashed outside. Far out at sea, they saw a dull white glow.

"It was the first time," recalled Hartman, "that we knew the war was coming home to us."

To the south, on the exclusive Jupiter Island community, windows cracked and dishes rattled.

"After 150 seconds, two detonations, under the bridge and astern in the engine room, where the sparks fly around the air," U-504 commander Fritz Poske noted in German in his war diary, later translated by historians.

The engine room blast killed five of the 34 crewmen. Explosions tore a gaping hole in the hull. Within minutes the crew was in two lifeboats, so quickly one left his false teeth behind. Residents later determined the powerful shock wave on land, the one that shook people in their beds on Jupiter Island, had come from a torpedo that missed the *Republic* and slammed into the reef.

In one lifeboat, Captain Alfred Anderson, a 36-year veteran of the sea, saw the sub pass. The crew waited to be riddled by gunfire or blown out of the water. The sub approached the lifeboat, apparently determined it was not signaling anyone, and slipped away. One lifeboat was picked up by a ship. About three hours later, the other boat came ashore at Jupiter Island, behind two homes owned by part-time residents. Neighbors gave them dry clothes and food and drink. Their recovery was going a little too well by the time Captain Anderson arrived. He sobered them up quickly by reminding them of the ordeal they had endured and the deaths of their comrades. They filed onto waiting U.S. Navy trucks for a West Palm Beach hotel.

The ship settled a short distance from where it was hit, on a reef in about forty feet of water about five miles east of Hobe Sound. Its stern sat on the bottom and its bow jutted high above the surface. It leaned 40 degrees on one side, too dangerous an angle for salvage. Two Jupiter residents boarded the *Republic* the next day and found a terrified wire-haired terrier named Dolly. It was later reunited with its owner, the ship's quartermaster. Two days after it was hit, the ship broke up and disappeared. The U-boat was sunk 17 months later off Spain with no survivors.

At about 5:25 a.m. February 22, about twenty miles off Melbourne as the 24-year-old, 8,103-ton *Cities Service Empire* hauled nearly four million gallons of Texas crude north toward Philadelphia without lights, one crewman invited another out of the radio room for a cup of coffee on deck. That saved both their lives. The submarine U-128, captained by Lt. Commander Ulrich Heyse and fresh off its kill of the *Pan Massachusetts*, surfaced and fired three torpedoes. All missed. Two more missed. The infuriated captain charged toward the tanker, which was drawing away. Two more torpedoes were fired. Three and a half minutes later, as seaman Frank Heap sat in his bunk, he heard two torpedoes slam into the *Empire's* hull in rapid-fire succession and a third a few seconds later. He struggled to the deck to find the starboard side in flames.

Crewmembers tried to reach a 5-inch gun mounted for security but the flames drove them back. The cook threw a scaffolding overboard and clung to it. Heap and other crewmembers clamored onto a life raft. They held it dangerously close to the burning ship long enough for a crewman to swim toward it, desperately trying to outrace the flames spreading across the water.

Fourteen of the crew of fifty died, including the captain, crushed between the hull and a lifeboat while trying to rescue another man. The survivors, some in shorts, waited 3-1/2 hours in the cold for help. Survivors were eventually picked up by a Navy destroyer, the *Biddle*, and a Coast Guard cutter.

"That evening about dusk, we got orders to unload the wounded and dead at Fort Pierce," recalled *Biddle* crewmember Herbert Goeler, now living in Boynton Beach, south of West Palm Beach. "You could see the buildings and the beaches, and the war was right there."

The 465-foot-long *Empire*, torn in two, went 250 feet to the bottom thirty-three miles east of the entrance to Port Canaveral. The U-boat was sunk off Brazil 15 months later.

My First Trip To Florida

At seven that same night, February 22, the 21-year-old, 10,277-ton *W.D. Anderson* was heading north 12 miles north of Jupiter with a cargo of crude oil. The crew was at chow. Two men had already eaten and were on watch at the back of the 500-foot ship, swapping tales. One was Frank Leonard Terry, 23, the ship's "wiper;" he was an apprentice who helped tend the boilers and watch for steam leaks. Terry was sipping coffee when a torpedo hit the engine room with a dull thud. It was from U-504, killer of the *Republic*.

"The ship stood, in a fraction of a second, from forward to astern in flames," German commander Poske wrote. "After 12 seconds, second (torpedo) hits in the stern; the rear part broke off."

Terry jumped over a railing and dove into the water.

"I was in the air when the second torpedo hit," recalled Terry, now in his late 80s and a retired steelworker and part-time security guard who lives in Parkesburg, Pennsylvania, near Philadelphia. "I thought my insides were going to fall out."

The second strike sprayed oil that coated the plummeting Terry and covered the surface when he came up for air.

"There was heavy smoke all 'round and fire. I heard a lot of screaming and hollering. I could feel heat and smoke. I tried to get away from it."

Terry dragged a shipmate through the water, then had to let him go. He yelled for the man to follow him away from the flame and swam as fast as he could.

"All I heard was a big scream. He was on fire. Poor guy burned up."

Terry swam under the inferno until he thought his lungs would burst, finally surfacing clear. He could see the ship begin to sink in 240 feet of water. He was in the freezing water with no shirt or shoes, only his pants. He could find nothing to hang onto and treaded water for three hours, coated in oil. He shouted in vain into the dark and empty night. He saw only the light of the burning ship and heard the sounds of five separate explosions. Then, just when he feared he couldn't last five minutes more, a rescue boat loomed. Terry yelled and waved, terrified it would miss him in the darkness. Finally, its spotlight fell on him. Terry insisted to rescuers that sharks had bitten off his legs until they showed him his numb limbs. He was taken to Stuart, the only survivor out of thirty-six men.

"It was my first trip to Florida. I didn't like the experience. When I finally thought of my pals, they were in my prayers. I was a nervous wreck. The Germans? I figure it was war. It was their duty."

Local media covered the sinkings of the *Empire* and *Republic* but had to wait two days for the federal Office of Censorship to clear publication. A note assured Palm Beach *Post* readers the paper was on the job but hampered by government, reminding them, "If it's anything we can't print, you shouldn't be talking about it."

A Deadly May

On April 3, the *Gulf State* was sunk off Key West. The tanker, taking crude oil from Corpus Christi, Texas to Portland, Maine, took torpedoes in rapid order—one under the bridge and one in the engine room—at about 3:15 a.m. The fire broke out so quickly there was no time to break out boats or rafts. The ship sank in five minutes. Only eighteen of the crew of forty-eight was saved; survivors jumped off and swam through debris and flaming oil; some survivors clung to a raft that had been thrown free. Rescuers picked up survivors and some dead about noon and took them to Key West. One crewmember, James F. Harrell, received the Merchant Marine Distinguished Service Medal "for the heroism which cost his life."

On April 10, the *Gulf America* went down off Jacksonville. The ship, carrying furnace oil, was hit about 10:20 p.m. by two torpedoes. The captain immediately gave the order to abandon ship. As the crew did so, the sub surfaced and began to shell the *Gulf America*, throwing the evacuation into chaos. Of thirty-eight crewmembers, twenty-nine survivors were picked up in lifeboats several hours later and brought to a base at Mayport, near Jacksonville. Twelve bodies were retrieved from the water. The remaining seven were presumed lost. The ship settled on the bottom and some papers were retrieved; six days later it turned over and sank from sight.

Two more ships would go down in April. On April 12, the *Leslie*, a freighter hauling 3,300 tons of sugar from Cuba to New York, was sunk by U-123 five to 15 miles off Cape Canaveral. Four of 32 crewmembers died. On April 13 the *Korsholm*, a freighter with 4,953 tons of phosphate, was hit by gunfire from U-123 four miles from the *Leslie*. Nine of 26 crewmembers died.

But the deadliest stretch came in May, when 10 ships sank in 10 days.

May 1: the *La Paz*, a freighter, was hit by U-109 off Cape Canaveral. All 57 aboard survived.

May 3, 2:15 a.m.: the *Ocean Venus*, a freighter hauling lead and lumber, was sunk by U-564 off Melbourne. The crew fired on the sub, then abandoned ship. Five of 47 crewmembers died. And about an hour and a half later, at 4:55 a.m. on May 3, the *Laertes*, a freighter hauling 5,020 tons of airplanes, tanks and trucks, was hit twice in four minutes off Cape Canaveral by U-109. Eighteen of 66 crewmembers died. The same day, U-506 struck the *Sami*.

Then, at 1 p.m. on May 4, the British tanker *Eclipse*, bearing aviation fuel, was southbound for Texas a mile off Boynton Inlet, about halfway between West Palm Beach and Boca Raton. It never expected a torpedo from the direction of land, but U-564 had maneuvered between it and the coast a few hundred yards away. The second officer saw the torpedo's wake. "Hard a-starboard!" he shouted. Five seconds later the ship was lifted six feet by the blast. Two men below were killed. Twenty-nine boarded lifeboats and were taken by rescue ships to Boynton Inlet. Sixteen stayed with the *Eclipse*, which was later towed to Port Everglades in Fort Lauderdale. The ship's master, a veteran of three previous attacks, was grateful to have cheated death again.

At 11 o'clock that night, near Jupiter Island, as the freighter *DeLisle* headed south from Baltimore to Puerto Rico with 2,000 tons of cargo, much of it camouflage paint, U-564 struck again. A crewman spotted the torpedo heading from shore 300 feet away. Seconds later there was a 40-foot hole in the ship's side and two dead men in the engine room. Thirty crewmembers and four Puerto Rican stowaways later rowed ashore. The *DeLisle* rested near shore, not far from the *Republic*. A Jupiter man stood watch on the ship for five lonely nights. On the second night, he looked below and saw a white form float back and forth as the ship rocked. It was the body of one of the two engine room crewmen. The second body was recovered the next day.

At 11:45 p.m. on May 5, U-333 commander Peter Cremer targeted the *Java Arrow*, silhouetted by the moon off Fort Pierce as the 21-year-old, 8,327-ton ship sailed south for South Africa with 1,400 tons of oil and drinking water. Two torpedoes struck a minute apart, leading to speculation there were two subs. The first hit below the bridge; the second entered the engine room, killing two officers. The 45 survivors were taken to Fort Pierce and Miami.

"Twelve hours later, we still saw smoke all across the horizon," Cremer wrote.

The burned hulk was towed ninety hours to Port Everglades and was later salvaged.

Four hours after sinking the *Java Arrow*, U-333 found another victim. The Dutch freighter *Amazone* was off Hobe Sound at 3:40 a.m. May 6, northbound to New York on a moonlit night with 900 tons of coffee, sisal fiber, orange peel, oil burners and mail. Two officers on the deck saw a dark shape behind them. A torpedo ripped into the ship, sending flames to the top of the mast. Fourteen men went down with the ship in minutes in 80 feet.

"The boat sank like a stone," Cremer wrote. The wreck remains in 75 to 100 feet of water about 10 miles off the St. Lucie Nuclear Power Plant near Fort Pierce. Nine men clung to a capsized lifeboat; another 11 grabbed rafts and debris. Drifting with the current, they passed the ominous shadow of the U-boat. Three hours after the attack, they were picked up and taken to Miami.

At 4:55 a.m., U-333 claimed its third kill in a little more than five hours. The U-boat had moved just offshore near Jupiter Island so merchant ships would not see it silhouetted against the moon or the sunrise. It sent two torpedoes out to the 7,000-ton *Halsey*, northbound to New York with nearly 3-1/2 million gallons of oil. At least one torpedo ripped a 60-foot hole in the ship. Within 15 minutes, the crew of thirty-two, swooning from oil fumes and terrified of an explosion, had taken to the lifeboats. A tanker that came alongside to pick them up fell into U-333's sights, but the torpedo jammed in the tube, robbing Cremer of a fourth kill. Two U.S. ships flung depth charges and chased the U-boat, but it outran them. The *Halsey*'s survivors were taken to Gilbert's Bar House of Refuge on Hutchinson Island, near Stuart. At 6 a.m., the ship, water breaking over its bridge, was suddenly torn in half by a horrific explosion in its middle, caused perhaps by a flare on a lifeboat. It sank in 50 feet of water some sixteen miles north of Jupiter and eight miles offshore, its mast visible and flames still spewing from it and roiling on the surface.

Two days later, at 13 minutes past noon on May 8, U-564 made a daring daylight attack on the *Ohioan*. The ship was northbound several miles off Boca Raton with 6,000 tons of ore, 1,300 tons of licorice root and 300 tons of wool. The ship instantly tilted to the left as crewmen scrambled over the side. There was no time to take to lifeboats, which were torn from the ship as it sank. It went down in two minutes in 550 feet of water, sucking several seamen down with it. Fifteen of the thirty-seven crewmembers were lost; survivors swam to the scattered boats and were later picked up and taken to West Palm Beach.

At 3:20 a.m. on May 9, 3-1/2 miles east of Delray Beach, U-564 made another strike. The *Lubrafol*, sailing north from Aruba to New York with 2-1/2 million gallons of fuel oil, took a torpedo, perhaps two. A fuel tank burst into flame and a mast toppled. Two crewmembers were killed. The remaining forty-two dashed to lifeboats; one boat caught fire and panicked seamen jumped into the water and were lost. A Coast Guard cutter pulled the three boats away from the fire, landing them later at Boynton Inlet. Thirteen of the 44 crewmen were dead or missing. The ship drifted away and eventually sank.

The killing continued:

May 1: The *Worden*, off Melbourne.

May 3: The *Sama*, east of Hollywood.

May 4: The *Norlindo*, off Key West.

Also May 4: The *Munger T. Ball*, torpedoed twice in 30 seconds, at 6:40 p.m. about 100 miles northwest of the Dry Tortugas. The American tanker was believed to be hauling gasoline from Port Arthur, Texas, to Wilmington, N.C. The ship sank within 50 minutes. Survivors said the ship was moving about six miles per hour when it was struck. The first explosion hit the port side, and the ship burst into flames. After the second torpedo struck, the U-boat surfaced and began to machine-gun the tanker from end to end. The crew tried to free lifeboats, but the fire had stuck their latches tight, and the men shimmied down ropes into the water. Four men were picked up by another ship and brought to Key West. The remaining twenty-nine were presumed lost. Survivors could not say whether any distress calls were sent, and authorities believe any confidential documents went down with the *Ball*.

Nine miles north of the *Ball*, the crew of the *Joseph M. Cudahy* saw the ship burst into flame and tried to steer clear of danger after radioing about the *Ball*. Crewmembers said they believed a sub was tailing them; about 9:30, the conning tower of a U-boat was spotted 500 feet off starboard. Seconds later, a torpedo slammed into the ship, and fire broke out immediately. The ship's master steered into the wind; he and eight others climbed into a boat. The nine, and another plucked from the water, were taken about 9:00 a.m. to Key West. The other twenty-seven men aboard were presumed killed. Three days later, the tanker, gutted and still burning, was spotted by another ship. Because the *Cudahy* was a threat to other vessels, the second ship sank it with gunfire.

U-564 wasn't done. The *Portero Del Llano*, eight miles off Miami Beach, went down May 13. And on July 7, U-571 struck the *Umtata*.

The *J.A. Moffett Jr.* was moving in 24 feet of water, about six miles southwest of Long Key, south of Key Largo, just after midnight on July 8. When the first torpedo hit, the ship nosed into the reef and grounded. A second torpedo hit near the engine room. The ship's master, badly hurt, was taken overboard, but crewmen lost him trying to launch the lifeboat; his body was later recovered. The remaining forty-three crewmembers got into lifeboats. About 1:00 a.m., the U-boat surfaced and shelled the boat; it was gutted by fire. The crew was picked up about 3:00 a.m. and taken to Craig Key. The *Moffett* was later pulled off the reef and towed to Galveston, Texas for repairs.

At about 1:30 a.m. on July 15, the *Pennsylvania Sun* was hit west of the Dry Tortugas when a patrol plane flew over it, brightly lighting it — probably to spot it for its attacker. Within minutes, the first torpedo struck, instantly killing two lookouts and spraying oil, which caught fire. The ship's master said to keep the ship moving, but someone without authorization tripped the emergency switch, and the ship came to a dead stop. The master then called to abandon ship. The remaining fifty-seven crewmembers were picked up 3-1/2 hours later and taken to Key West. The next day, four officers returned to the *Sun* with a salvage tug and put out the last stubborn fires, The ship was towed to Key West and eventually moved to Pennsylvania for an overhaul.

Tapering Off

By mid-May of 1942, the United States finally instituted convoys. Destroyers, sub chasers and other small military boats escorted the ships, their gray shapes moving slowly and silently across the horizon. The attacks tapered off. There were only four off Florida in 1943 and none in 1944 and 1945.

Ironically, the deadliest disaster of the war was caused only indirectly by the Germans. Two ships under wartime orders to travel without lights collided off Jupiter Inlet just before 11 p.m. on October 20, 1943. The empty *Gulf Bell*, torpedoed once before and salvaged, rammed the *Gulfland*, filled with gasoline. The sea became an inferno. Of 116 seamen on the two ships, eighty-eight died. The *Gulf Bell* ran aground. As in the *Republic*, rescuers later found a singed dog aboard. The *Gulfland* burned off Hobe Sound for a remarkable seven weeks. It lit the night sky as authorities watched helplessly, held back by flames that singed their hair and curled paint on the ship. Later, workers were able to poke holes in the *Gulfland* and it sank in 30 feet of water. A year after the accident, salvagers made a grim discovery on the *Gulfland* – the bones of 15 men who had desperately sought refuge in a shower. The stern was moved off but the bow remains at the bottom, where it is a popular diving spot.

By war's end, the Allies had sunk many U-boats, but apparently none off Florida. A 1945 U.S. Navy report said the Coast Guard cutter *Nike* "probably" sank a U-boat off the Jupiter lighthouse on May 18, 1942. The cutter dropped depth charges that sent geysers of water and foam high in the air. The sub surfaced and headed south, under full power but badly damaged, judging from a heavy oil slick that trailed it.

"A continuing oil slick gave evidence of the probable destruction of the enemy vessel," said a citation recognizing the cutter for its actions. But neither U.S. nor German reports documented any such sinking.

Legacy Of Death

Operation Drumbeat had left its legacy: a line of ships lying on the bottom, cargo strewn on the ocean floor and oil oozing from ruptured tanks. The success of the U-boats spurred a new push for the Cross-Florida Barge Canal, a route across the northern peninsula that was finally started in the 1960s and later abandoned as an environmental disaster. The militarization of Florida also left its mark. Many bases were transformed to public use. Soldiers heading home from the front got heroes' welcomes as their trains passed through West Palm Beach.

"Our mayor called me and asked me to rush down to the West Palm Beach train station and tell a train full of servicemen coming from Miami that the war was over and we had won!" recalled Frances Stambaugh, who was Miss West Palm Beach of 1945. A newspaper photograph shows her, an American flag at her shoulder, displaying a newspaper with "PEACE!" in a gigantic headline. A beaming soldier holding a bottle hangs out a train window.

"It was one of the most exciting moments of my life to see the joy on the faces of those men," she said.

Those men, and those who had been stationed in South Florida, went home with stories of the paradise they had left. Many later returned for good.

"A lot of the population explosion has come later, and was not directly connected to the war, but it was the growth after the war that really touched that all off," said Rodney Dillon of Fort Lauderdale's Broward County Historical Commission.

That boom continues today. New residents in their condominiums and beach chairs gaze at a peaceful sea. They are unaware that not so long ago, it was a place of terror and death.

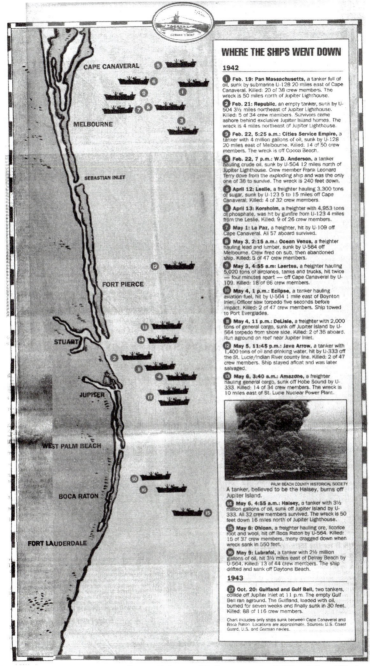

WHERE THE SHIPS WENT DOWN

1942

1 **Feb. 19: Pan Massachusetts**, a tanker full of oil, sunk by submarine U-128 20 miles east of Cape Canaveral. Killed: 20 of 38 crew members. The wreck is 50 miles north of Jupiter Lighthouse.

2 **Feb. 21: Republic**, an empty tanker, sunk by U-504 3½ miles northeast of Jupiter Lighthouse. Killed: 5 of 34 crew members. Survivors came ashore behind exclusive Jupiter Island homes. The wreck is 4 miles northeast of Jupiter Lighthouse.

3 **Feb. 22, 5:25 a.m.: Cities Service Empire**, a tanker with 4 million gallons of oil, sunk by U-128 20 miles east of Melbourne. Killed: 14 of 50 crew members. The wreck is off Cocoa Beach.

4 **Feb. 22, 7 p.m.: W.D. Anderson**, a tanker hauling crude oil, sunk by U-504 12 miles north of Jupiter Lighthouse. Crew member Frank Leonard Terry dove from the exploding ship and was the only one of 36 to survive. The wreck is 240 feet down.

5 **April 12: Leslie**, a freighter hauling 3,300 tons of sugar, sunk by U-123 5 to 15 miles off Cape Canaveral. Killed: 4 of 32 crew members.

6 **April 13: Korsholm**, a freighter with 4,953 tons of phosphate, was hit by gunfire from U-123 4 miles from the Leslie. Killed: 9 of 26 crew members.

7 **May 1: La Paz**, a freighter, hit by U-109 off Cape Canaveral. All 57 aboard survived.

8 **May 3, 2:15 a.m.: Ocean Venus**, a freighter hauling lead and lumber, sunk by U-564 off Melbourne. Crew fired on sub, then abandoned ship. Killed: 5 of 47 crew members.

9 **May 3, 4:55 a.m.: Laertes**, a freighter hauling 5,020 tons of airplanes, tanks and trucks, hit twice — four minutes apart — off Cape Canaveral by U-109. Killed: 18 of 66 crew members.

10 **May 4, 1 p.m.: Eclipse**, a tanker hauling aviation fuel, hit by U-564 1 mile east of Boynton Inlet. Officer saw torpedo five seconds before impact. Killed: 2 of 47 crew members. Ship towed to Port Everglades.

11 **May 4, 11 p.m.: DeLisle**, a freighter with 2,000 tons of general cargo, sunk off Jupiter Island by U-564 torpedo from shore side. Killed: 2 of 36 aboard. Run aground on reef near Jupiter Inlet.

12 **May 5, 11:45 p.m.: Java Arrow**, a tanker with 1,400 tons of oil and drinking water, hit by U-333 off the St. Lucie/Indian River county line. Killed: 2 of 47 crew members. Ship stayed afloat and was later salvaged.

13 **May 6, 3:40 a.m.: Amazone**, a freighter hauling general cargo, sunk off Hobe Sound by U-333. Killed: 14 of 34 crew members. The wreck is 10 miles east of St. Lucie Nuclear Power Plant.

PALM BEACH COUNTY HISTORICAL SOCIETY
A tanker, believed to be the Halsey, burns off Jupiter Island.

14 **May 6, 4:55 a.m.: Halsey**, a tanker with 3½ million gallons of oil, sunk off Jupiter Island by U-333. All 32 crew members survived. The wreck is 50 feet down 16 miles north of Jupiter Lighthouse.

15 **May 8: Ohioan**, a freighter hauling ore, licorice root and wool, hit off Boca Raton by U-564. Killed: 15 of 37 crew members, many dragged down when wreck sank in 550 feet.

16 **May 9: Lubrafol**, a tanker with 2½ million gallons of oil, hit 3½ miles east of Delray Beach by U-564. Killed: 13 of 44 crew members. The ship drifted and sank off Daytona Beach.

1943

17 **Oct. 20: Gulfland and Gulf Bell**, two tankers, collide off Jupiter Inlet at 11 p.m. The empty Gulf Bell ran aground. The Gulfland, loaded with oil, burned for seven weeks and finally sunk in 30 feet. Killed: 88 of 116 crew members.

Chart includes only ships sunk between Cape Canaveral and Boca Raton. Locations are approximate. Sources: U.S. Coast Guard, U.S. and German navies.

German U-boats sank twenty-four ships off the coast of Florida. Sixteen of them were sunk between Cape Canaveral and Boca Raton during the four months of February through March 1942. (Map courtesy of Pat Crowley, Palm Beach *Post* staff artist)

CHAPTER 3

Bread Wrappers and Theater Tickets

Various urban legends and folk tales that sprang up during the desperate war years have since been discounted. Among them:

- A submarine crew was captured and brought ashore at Jupiter Inlet, where a Marine unit sent them to a prisoner-of-war camp in Kentucky.
- A group of cold and miserable Germans came ashore at Palm Beach and surrendered on a residential street. (This may be a variation of the Jupiter Inlet tale.)
- A crew was captured and held for authorities in the downtown West Palm Beach Burdines department store.
- A watchman on the old Palm Beach pier heard clanging, banging and German voices in the dark and fired blindly, apparently scaring them off. Three days later, the body of a German seaman, killed by a gunshot, washed ashore in the Boca Raton area.
- The George Washington Hotel in downtown West Palm Beach was owned by a German family. Red lights installed on the roofs of all tall buildings warn airplanes landing at the nearby West Palm Beach airport. But these supposedly flashed in a sequence that messaged offshore subs.
- Carrier pigeons sent messages to subs.
- A Palm Beach woman and her Nazi butler hid a German submarine in an inlet of the Intracoastal Waterway behind her estate. The butler used a short-wave radio in the basement to lead U-boats to tankers and away from pursuers. An FBI agent and the former butler were killed when they learned too much. The FBI eventually uncovered the plan, killed the butler and arrested the matron, and ordered an aerial strike that destroyed the sub, apparently with no one on the woman's street seeing or hearing anything.

That story was published in 1985 in a Boca Raton magazine; editors' efforts to verify it apparently went no further than a note at the head saying that the author vouched for its authenticity.

- Subs would send parties ashore where "nests" of sympathizers would restock them with food.

- Germans came ashore to buy fresh groceries or attend movies. Searches of captured boats revealed American cigarettes, a bread wrapper from Florida's Holsum bakery, and tickets for a film at downtown Miami's Olympia theater, now the Gusman Center for the Performing Arts. (A North Carolina writer reports the same legends in his area, even down to mention of a local bakery and theater there.)

One man stuck to his story to his grave. Robert Salisbury, a Palm Beach attorney who died in 1989, said that during the Korean War, when he was an agent in the Air Force's Office of Special Investigations, he was shown a surveillance film that showed a black raft coming ashore after dark. The men changed from their black gear into civilian clothes. Using infrared photography, the camera, hidden in a car tailing them, followed them as they walked up a sidewalk and into a building with a sign that said *TaBoo*, the name of a Palm Beach nightspot. Salisbury says he was told the film was shot in Palm Beach in 1943 and that authorities told him the Germans were just coming ashore for cigarettes or recreation and were not captured for fear of creating a panic. Author Michael Gannon says Salisbury may have seen a training film—a reenactment used to train coast watchers. Gannon said U-boat commanders have told him no crew members ever left their subs except to rendezvous at sea to exchange code books or food or stretch refueling lines between boats. He said the boats were well stocked and it would have been considered the ultimate in stupidity to violate orders and risk capture just for American cigarettes or beer or a movie.

CHAPTER 4

The Invasion of Florida

Most rumors about Nazis sneaking onto Florida shores were just that. But it did happen once. In fact, when enemy saboteurs dropped off by U-boats slipped ashore in June 1942 at Ponte Vedra Beach, south of Jacksonville, and on New York's Long Island, it was the first "invasion" of the American mainland since the War of 1812.

Operation Pastorius, named for the first German immigrant in America, was terrorism in its art form—scattered mischief with dramatic results. The operatives would disperse across the continent and perform acts of sabotage on metal factories, railroads, and power and water plants. The nation would be scared witless.

Because the entire coastline was on alert in the wake of numerous sinkings by U-boats, American authorities were confident of detecting any enemy landing. They were wrong.

The German admiral who signed the orders for the mission was convinced "This will cost these poor men their lives." For six of the eight, he was right. By the end of the summer, they would go to the electric chair in the capital of the nation they hoped to defeat. Their capture came not by brilliant U.S. detective work but by the betrayal of their own.

The Mission

Once ashore, the two groups were to make their way to a Cincinnati hotel, linking up on the Fourth of July. From there they would go on to their targets: aluminum plants in Tennessee, East St. Louis, Ill., and Massena, N.Y.; New York's Hell Gate Bridge; a stretch of the Pennsylvania Railroad near Altoona, Pa. and its terminal in Newark, N.J.; a hydroelectric plant in Niagara Falls; and the water system of New York City. The secondary round of targets was aimed more at the psyches of the American people. Explosions at department stores and bus and rail terminals would terrorize and demoralize the public and the war effort. Unnerved citizens would target German-Americans, goading them into a united movement.

The Teams

The eight German marines picked for the mission had all lived and worked in the United States. Two were naturalized citizens.

The Florida team: Edward John Kerling, 33, had been a Brooklyn mechanic. He believed Americans looked down on him and saw a chance to further the master race of his birth. Herbert Hans Haupt, 22, an optical worker, had been brought to Chicago by his parents at age five. His father was a loyal Nazi and Haupt had drilled with the German American Bund. Werner Thiel, 35, had been a toolmaker in Detroit, Philadelphia and Los Angeles. Herman Neubauer, 32, had been a hotel worker in Hartford, and Chicago.

The Long Island team: Richard Quirin, 34; Heinrich Heinck, 35, Ernst Burger, 36, and their leader, Georg Johann Dasch, 39.

The eight were recruited and trained by a German-American intelligence officer. They attended a sabotage school near Berlin, getting crash training in explosive devices and boning up on American slang and hit songs. Each man was given a fake identity and the accompanying documents and taken to the Nazi sub base at Lorient, France. First they enjoyed a two-day stopover in Paris, where Haupt got into a midnight fight with a prostitute and Dasch blabbed about the mission to a bartender before ending the evening in a free-for-all fistfight with his fellow saboteurs.

The Landing

The teams landed at sites selected for being in the middle of nowhere.

The first four landed on June 12, 1942, at Amagansett, a small town just west of the very tip of Long Island.

U-584 landed the other four early on June 17 in Ponte Vedra Beach.

The four pulled ashore in a rubber raft. They wore swim shorts and official German marine caps bearing the eagle and swastika. If captured, they would demand to be considered prisoners of war. Disguised as civilians, they could be arrested as foreign spies and face the death penalty. They carried $170,000 in American currency to be used for expenses and to buy off acquaintances and relatives in America. They carried ashore four waterproof boxes, which they buried with plans to return for them later.

"There were curious bombs designed to look like lumps of coal," the Associated Press reported. "There were innocent-looking pen and pencil sets. There was incendiary material with which to convert the pens and pencils for firebombs... There were fuses, detonators and timing devices."

The four buried the explosives in sand dunes near an abandoned house two hundred feet east of State Road A1A. Once established in America, they would return by car to recover the materials.

`"It was estimated that the explosives and other equipment furnished these men when utilized in connection with their training in preparing additional explosives and incendiary material would last the saboteurs two years,'" a November 14, 1942 FBI report said. "They came to maim and kill,'" FBI Director J. Edgar Hoover would say.

No one paid attention to the four men playing in the surf with a beach ball. St. Johns County deputy Roy Landrum and his wife saw nothing suspicious about the customers at the general store and post office they owned three miles from the landing site. The four asked for matches and the schedule of buses to Jacksonville, then boarded a bus. Once in Jacksonville, they enjoyed a hearty breakfast, then registered in pairs at two downtown hotels. They then split up and headed out.

The Capture

On the wind-swept end of Long Island, an unarmed U.S. Coast Guardsman spotted the four spies. Georg Dasch tried to bribe him with $260. But the official ran off to report the four. By the time help arrived, they were gone. Thirty hours after the landing, Dasch called the New York office of the FBI. He said his name was Frank Daniel Pastorius and he wanted to report a major incident. The agent considered it a crank call.

Dasch then went to Washington and asked to meet with FBI director J. Edgar Hoover. He settled for a meeting with agents, who were convinced when he dropped $80,000 in cash in front of them. He told the agents of both teams of saboteurs. The Florida party had not yet landed.

Once arriving in Jacksonville, Kerling and Thiel had headed to New York. FBI agents tracked Kerling on June 24 to Central Park, where they watched as he embraced his mistress. They arrested him in a nearby bar. They then took him in cuffs and leg irons to Jacksonville, where he pointed out the buried explosives.

"It was a sight," former deputy and store owner Landrum recalled for a 50th anniversary story in *The Florida Times Union* in 1992. "They had enough stuff to wipe out factories and everything."

Haupt and Neubauer went to Chicago. Haupt was helped by his parents, other relatives, and a Chicago Bund member. He also spent time with a former girlfriend and a bartender; while he partied, the two turned him in. He was picked up at a roadside inn on June 27; those who had helped him were also arrested. Neubauer was picked up the same day at a Chicago hotel.

Soon, all eight had been rounded up.

The Trial

The eight Germans were charged with espionage, sabotage and conspiracy and tried by a military commission in Washington. The press was kept out. Fourteen others would also be tried for their roles in helping the saboteurs. The trial of the eight took three weeks. Dasch claimed he'd returned to Germany to visit his mother and was forced into espionage. Kerling refused to implicate the others. Haupt said he'd participated only out of fear. Thiel said he thought the sabotage school was a school for propagandists and wanted only to get back to America. Neubauer said he was doing his soldier's duty—just following orders.

All eight were convicted and sentenced to death by electrocution. President Franklin Roosevelt commuted Dasch's and Burger's sentences because of their cooperation. Burger got life at hard labor, Dasch, thirty years. The other six, including the four Florida operatives, died just after noon on August 8 in the District of Columbia's electric chair. It had been only eight weeks since they came ashore with plans to terrorize America.

In 1959, Dasch published a memoir, *Eight Spies Against America*. In it, he argued he had reluctantly returned to Germany at his mother's urging; he had never been more than a waiter and she told him he could find good work and that the war would probably be a short one. Dasch said he soon came face to face with the oppression of the Nazi machine and regretted his return. He found work translating foreign broadcasts for the Nazi government and soon dabbled with resistance operatives. When he was picked for the mission because of his knowledge of American geography and the English language, he instantly determined to go along with the mission in order to scuttle it. He even wrote a letter giving his serial number from his brief stint in the U.S. Army in the late 1920s and planned to give it to his mother to take to his sister in Switzerland, who would take it to the American embassy, but his mother vetoed the idea as too dangerous, Dasch wrote.

After giving himself up, Dasch said, he was double-crossed by the FBI, which wanted all the credit for breaking the case and didn't want the public to know a terrorist plot would have succeeded but for Dasch. In the closed military proceeding, the U.S. government argued Dasch turned only after getting cold feet—out of fear, rather than as part of a plan to trip up the Nazis. Instead of being made a hero, Dasch was sentenced to prison.

On March 20, 1948, President Harry Truman approved clemency for Dasch and Burger and the two were deported. "Upon receipt of custody the Secretary of the Army will effect their transportation to the American Zone of Occupied Germany," Truman wrote. "It is the view of the Department of Justice," Attorney General Tom C. Clark wrote, "that Burger and Dasch have now been sufficiently punished for their offenses against the United States." FBI records indicate a policy of "no return to the U.S.A. later."

In Germany, Dasch worked for years to find people who would back his story and help him clear his name. Meanwhile, the New York *Daily News*, quoting unidentified sources, backed Dasch's version. But in a 1959 *Newsweek* article about the book, former U.S. Attorney General Francis Biddle dismissed his claim, calling him "a damned liar."

In 1980, the Atlanta *Constitution*, citing trial transcripts, FBI reports and other documents obtained through the Freedom of Information Act, confirmed much of Dasch's version of events and the FBI's handling of him. He finally gave up seeking a pardon, but by then the German press had targeted him for betraying his fellow saboteurs and walking free while they had gone to the electric chair. He was hounded from town to town; once a man leaped from the shadows to kill him but faltered and fled. He died November 1, 1991, in Ludwigshafen, Germany.

In the 1960s, North Florida residents erected a marker to note *Operation Pastorius*. It was stolen in 1988, and a substitute was put up in the same spot. But in May 1991, the new one was stolen. The mayor of nearby Neptune Beach stumbled across the $1,200, 222-pound marker six months later in a cache of stolen banners, flags and street signs at an abandoned apartment in Atlantic Beach. The mayor, a real estate broker, had been inspecting the building for a prospective buyer. The marker was returned to its location in time for the 50th anniversary in 1992.

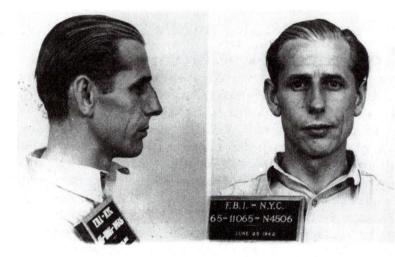

George Dasch insisted he joined the German sabotage unit only to ensure its failure. (Photo courtesy of the Palm Beach *Post*)

CHAPTER 5

The Military Bases

Florida claims the longest military bloodlines in America, stretching five centuries to St. Augustine's Spanish colonial militia. Teddy Roosevelt's Rough Riders waited out the Spanish-American War in Tampa. Naval aviation was born in Pensacola just before World War I. A young George Bush ran training flights over Lake Okeechobee. The Cuban missile crisis turned Florida into an armed camp, with trucks ferrying troops, tanks and missiles right down U.S. 1. And the Persian Gulf War was run by U.S. Central Command, headquartered at MacDill Air Force Base in Tampa.

Bob Hawk, a former Florida National Guard historian and a scholar of the state's military history through Spanish, British and American rule, provided some logical reasons and one big political one for why Florida and the rest of the South boast so many bases. *Logical*: Moderate climate and an abundance of open land and coastline. *Political*: U.S. senators and representatives in the South tended to get re-elected regularly in the early 20th century, building tenure and gaining seats on committees that decided where bases would go.

"When the pork barrel was up, the South inevitably got more than its fair share of bases," Hawk said.

The decisions made decades ago continue to have tremendous payoffs. It was during World War II that the number of bases in Florida exploded. After Pearl Harbor, the military moved quickly. In town after town, military airfields were converted from municipal airports or built from scratch. Prisoner-of-War camps were set up in the sugar-growing areas west along Lake Okeechobee and Germans were put to work harvesting cane. Oceanfront hotels were commandeered by the military. Palm Beach's historic Breakers became the Ream military hospital. The Biltmore Hotel in Coral Gables was loaned to the U.S. Coast Guard and virtually stripped; each room had two sets of double bunks.

Charlie Ellington of West Palm Beach worked at a downtown jewelry store.

"What I remember most were the many servicemen coming in to buy engagement rings," she said.

"They were bittersweet times," said Adeen Gately of West Palm Beach. "So many beautiful young men enjoying Florida, which they called paradise, yet going off to war."

"The boy who gave me my nickname, Micki, did not come back," said Micki Shaw Cox of Jupiter. "Neither did many of the boys we danced with. Fifty years later, I'm still singing. Wherever they are, I hope they are too! I know they live forever in my heart."

Boca Raton Army Air Field

In 1942 the government confiscated land owned by families in the nearby Yamato Colony and used it for the Boca Raton Army Air Field, paying less than it was worth, according to family members. The military tore down barns, chicken sheds and outhouses at Yamato and used the rubble for a 500-yard-long obstacle course. While some historians say the two Japanese families remaining from the turn-of-the-century farming colony were exploited because of the national anti-Japanese sentiment, landowners not of Asian descent have also complained of being shortchanged at other military sites.

Boca Raton Army Air Field was formed as an Army Air Corps training site and radar training base. The property was later split; half became a municipal airport and the other half Florida Atlantic University. Former runways are now student parking lots.

Not everyone killed in wars dies in war. On the morning of May 12, 1944, nine men were killed when the light bomber they were flying crashed and burned during a routine takeoff. The dead, according to published reports: the pilot, 1st Lt. William H. Carson, Orangeburg, S.C.; 1st Lt. Jacob M. Bule, Inverness, Fla.; 1st Lt. Thomas A. Lamont, Mt. Vernon, N.Y.; 1st Lt. John J. Lominac, Asheville, N.C.; 1st Lt. Benjamin P. Sibley, Worcester, Mass.; Pfc. Norman R. Stiner, New York; Sgt. John J. Sasieko, Kenosha, Wisc.; Pfc. Robert E. Locke, Lewisburg, Ohio; S-Sgt. Frank L. Bursaw, St. Louis.

According to the Army's investigative report, the plane got only about 3,500 feet down the runway and about 40 feet off the ground before it swerved violently and went into almost a vertical bank. The left wing tip touched the ground and the plane made a sickening cartwheel onto its nose, twisting along its axis until it was almost 60 degrees upside down. As the plane burst into flames, the fuselage broke off just behind the main door and the right and left engines were each thrown ten feet; the plane went about another two hundred feet before it stopped.

Morrison Field

In 1940, Morrison Field was leased to the U.S. Army, which began building an Army air base. More land was bought, expanding the airport to 1,825 acres. A 1940 Works Progress Administration project expanded runways and taxiways. On February 27, 1941, the field officially became an Army post, although civilian air traffic continued. When Pearl Harbor was attacked December 7, 1941, people rushed to action half a world away in West Palm Beach. The Morrison Field Army Air Force Command was activated.

"The base was like a swarm of bees," Louis Zorzi, who managed the field's officer's club during the war, said in a 1977 interview. Zorzi died in February 1994. When Pearl Harbor was attacked, he said, "all hell broke loose out there. They didn't waste time. Things happened so quick. When war was declared, all the GIs were put on trains and shuttled out like that. I was the only one left."

A little more than a month later, on January 19, 1942, the Air Transport Command began operation. The army bought still more land, increasing the airport to 2,270 acres. Runways and other facilities were built, expanded or renovated, and water and sewer service brought in. During the war, about 3,000 people were stationed at the field. Virtually every U.S. bomber destined for battle flew out of West Palm Beach, and about 45,000 fighters trained at or left from Morrison Field. About 6,000 planes passed through in the eight months before D-Day. And the base maintained many giant C-54 cargo planes that "flew the hump" to supply Chinese fighting the Japanese invasion.

Zorzi, a Pennsylvania native who'd moved down in 1938, was working at a restaurant when he landed a job at the air field, managing the complex that included the officers' quarters, bachelor officers' quarters and club house. He was kept busy organizing activities and preparing for visits by dignitaries that included the Duke of Windsor and Chiang Kai Shek. Zorzi said he never saw a fight break out among the men.

"They were a good gang," said Zorzi's wife, Dorothy, who also worked at the club. "Knowing that there was a war on, it was amazing to see their spirit, their good morale. Some of the fliers had the feeling, 'Maybe this is my last trip.'"

"It was a tough thing to handle," Zorzi said from his home a few miles east of the airport. "It was nerve-wracking. You had them coming and going."

"Recollections of a soldier," from Emmett Toft, now living in Port St. Lucie, near Fort Pierce: "The tent city across the landing field from Morrison Field's front gate...the mosquito netting on each bunk...the road that paralleled the canal, full of gators, and in the distance you could see nothing but scrub and swamp."

Girls would be encouraged to come out to base dances and dance with the men.

"I was in my early 20s when 'the boys' arrived to activate the new Army Air Corps base at Morrison Field in 1941," recalled Kay Hutchins of West Palm Beach. "When 3,000 young men hit town, it was a bonanza beyond compare for single girls!"

The long hours and seven-day week were a strain on the Zorzis, and they finally left the base after the war ended.

"We had relations and what-nots in there, and it was hard to walk out and quit," Zorzi recalled.

On June 30, 1947, the U.S. Army Air Force, successor to the Army Air Corps, deactivated Morrison Field. A year later, it gave the airport back to Palm Beach County. On August 11, 1947, county commissioners changed the name to Palm Beach International Airport, a change that became official September 27, 1948. Residents soon came to know the big red neon sign that guided motorists to the new terminal, which opened December 17, 1947. The airport had its own eight-man fire department and housed sixty-five to seventy families, most living in former barracks that were converted to apartments for the military. Also among the buildings on the airport property was the fledgling Palm Beach Junior College, as well as a shoe store, a bed-maker, a fishing tackle shop and the State Welfare Board. And in the summer of 1949, visitors praised the modern control tower, complete with something called air conditioning.

In 1953, war loomed again, this time in the Far East. On April 29 that year, the county returned the airport to the federal government, which reactivated it. Some 5,000 troops were stationed there. A 10-1/2-acre site was reserved for a commercial aviation terminal. As the 1950s came to a close, the field was used by training crews from two new entities—the U.S. Air Force and the Strategic Air Command. But officials found the work of the military at Morrison Field could be done elsewhere. It was deactivated again on July 1, 1959, and the county took control. On March 22, 1961, it officially became county property. In 1962, talk of reactivation emerged during the Cuban missile crisis, but such talk died away quickly.

Camp Murphy

The white sands of Jonathan Dickinson State Park hold a history both ethereal and tangible. The 16-square-mile park's name honors the ordeal three centuries ago of the shipwrecked Jonathan Dickinson and his family, who walked adjacent beaches en route to St. Augustine and rescue. Its more current history can be found in the sand itself; spent bullet shells dating back to the park's incarnation as Camp Murphy, a strategic World War II training site.

Jonathan Dickinson, a Quaker merchant traveling from Jamaica to Philadelphia with his wife and 6-month-old son, was stranded with two-dozen other passengers when the ship on which they were riding, the *Reformation*, was beached on nearby Jupiter Island in 1696. Natives threatened to kill the party, then relented. For the next two months, Dickinson and his family trudged on a trek or more than 200 miles through the Florida wilderness. They eventually made their way to Philadelphia. Dickinson later published *Jonathan Dickinson's Journal*, a story of faith and determination that is also considered one of the most important eyewitness accounts of the original Indians, long ago exterminated by European aggression and disease.

Two and a half centuries later, when World War II broke out, the military came to Florida looking for land to place installations. The Reed family of Jupiter Island, owners of the Hobe Sound Co. real estate business, turned over 1,000 acres provided it be restored to its natural state after the Army was done with it. The Army also bought about 17 acres from the DuBois family, Jupiter pioneers dating back to the turn of the century, for $1,000. In a winding nine-mile path between U.S. 1 and the Florida East Coast Railway tracks, the Army threw together more than 1,000 buildings. The installation was named for Colonel William Herbert Murphy, a Signal Corps officer and radio pioneer who died in battle February 3, 1942. From 1942 to 1945, more than 10,000 men moved through the camp; as many as 6,000 were there at one time, giving the site a larger population than the nearby town of Jupiter. One cartoon called Camp Murphy the "poor man's West Point." Soldiers were there for the clandestine Southern Signal Corps School, where they learned the new concept of radar maintenance and operation. They were permitted to tell friends only that they were "in radio school." Many classes were at night.

"Say little and when in doubt remain QUIET!" says a note in the July 2, 1943 edition of the camp newsletter, the *Camp Murphy Message*. "You have a great secret. All great secrets are for the chosen few. Please keep it away from the many who would destroy you."

That same issue of the *Message* raved about the original comedy *On the Ball* — co-produced, co-written and co-directed by 19-year-old Sidney Lumet, later to become a acclaimed film director of such films as *Serpico, Prince of the City* and *The Verdict*. Despite only six weeks in preparation and rehearsal, the three-act play, which featured six original songs, "was a distinct hit and brought down the house," the newsletter said, "About 1,000 G.I's jammed the hall, sitting, standing and hanging from the rafters! It was easily the best thing of its kind ever done by Murphy actors." Lumet said through a spokeswoman that he doesn't remember much of his stay at Camp Murphy.

Jupiter pioneer and historian Bessie Wilson DuBois recalled how she, her husband and her three teenaged daughters all found work at the installation. She would arise at 2:00 a.m. to bake pies for her husband to take to the camp. The base theater featured *Going My Way* and *Double Indemnity*. Soldiers also found entertainment and companionship at USO clubs in Stuart and Jupiter and the DuBois restaurant, which featured a jukebox, piano and ping-pong. The Army would give rides to local girls to dances at the base.

Camp Murphy was deactivated in October 1944 and radar training returned to a site in New Jersey, although part of Murphy was operated by the U.S. Air Force and NASA into the 1960s. Most of the property was turned over to the state to become the park. The theater became a trash dump, the finance center a garage. In 1947, a concrete water reservoir was converted into offices; later, it became an emergency operations center for a nation cowering in fear of a nuclear war. It operated from 1953 to 1985, when emergency managers turned it over to the state. It is now the park office. Over the years, the camp's mess hall, chapel, many of the barracks and even the latrines were sold off and became cottages, warehouses and other building scattered across the Treasure Coast.

CHAPTER 6

The Medal Bill Murden Never Got

William Jesse Murden, an attorney, judge and mayor in Peekskill, N.Y., about 40 miles north of New York City, died at seventy-five on November 1, 1998. During a visit several years ago to his old army base, he mentioned to the Boca Raton Historical Society the incident that follows. On their request, he wrote up his account of what happened; he repeated the effort for this book. The following is a blend of his notes. Inquiries to military archives failed to uncover a report of the incident, although it is attested to not only by Murden, but by others, and was written up in the base newspaper, as repeated below. As with other incidents, archivists warn they have reports on 30,000 different crashes but believe there were far more. Record-keeping and cross-indexing were medieval compared with today's technology. And, with a war going on, some crashes were just never written up. It now appears clear that Murden's superior simply never got around to writing up a request for his act of bravery to be honored.

His Story

In February 1945, I had been in the Air Corps about two years and I was working as an aircraft and engine mechanic on the flight line at Boca Raton Army Air Base in Florida. This field was involved in training radar technicians and used both B-17s and B-24s in the flight training phases. My job was to take care of the planes that were used. They had the work set up at that time on a sort of an assembly-line scheme so that I found myself on the left inboard engine removing and replacing the spark plugs. Work was organized on the apron immediately in front of the hangars so that it progressed from station to station with the mechanics like myself remaining practically in place throughout the shift period.

At about 6:00 a.m. on a day in late February we were working under lights using 12-foot wooden stands built to fit the plane heights so that a swarm of men were able to simultaneously accomplish their separate tasks when I saw a tremendous flash of fire right about where I knew the field runways came together. That was about a half mile or so away. It just so happened that about then there was a lull at my station so I simply dropped everything and ran like hell through the palmetto and sand to see what was happening. I was no track star but I still made pretty good time considering it was predawn darkness with no defined pathway. Nevertheless, when I puffed up to the scene of the action I found myself late in getting there by a good two hundred men. Huge flames illuminated the scene and the great crowd that had been attracted by what it developed was an ill-advised attempt by two planes to take off using the same runway (the middle one) with one of them starting at right angles to the other but with neither being aware of the other's presence or intentions.

How such a thing could happen in view of all the procedures and safeguard practices the Air Corps constantly adhered to I to this day don't understand, but it happened. There were about ten men in each plane and even as I got there already it was being remarked by all that apparently nobody was even hurt, much less killed. At this point, as I was watching the raging fire consuming the B-17, with the B-24 engines still burning full bore but a couple of these minus a prop blade, or several prop blades, and with the planes only about twenty feet apart, I was astonished by the appearance of a civilian with a big flashlight in his hand. This disheveled gentleman slid out from under the bomb bay of the '24 and shouted, "Does anybody know how to cut off these motors?" He was talking about the engines of the B-24 which were four in number but two of them had only partial propellers and were winding up to about six or seven thousand revs, making a screaming noise along with the other two.

I naturally expected a surge of experts to come forward. None did. I heard myself say I knew how to do that, and the next thing I knew I was inside the B-24 alone—the man with the light having stepped out of my way. I stepped under the broken bomb-bay door and crawled up the slanting catwalk. I ran up to where the cabin of the B-24 would have been if it had not been crushed by the force of the crash with the other plane. The other plane was a B-17 and it was in the last throes of being consumed by flames. Miraculously the B-24, notwithstanding it had been the cause of the fire on itself, apparently did not ignite the B-24. The B-24 had a collapsed right landing gear and two propellers were missing although the engines were still screaming. The two right-hand engines were also going at high revs. The big thing was the cabin was almost completely crushed down so I had to crawl on top of the pilot's seat and throttle assemblies to reach any of the controls. I reached the controls by lying on top of the assemblies and proceeded to yank all four throttles back at the same time I cut all the engines and silence reigned. It was truly deafening. Also, all the cabin lights, which had been furnishing what light besides firelight there was, were out with a capital "O." Suddenly it was black inside with what looked like raw flame all around. I had the sudden urge to leave the premises. But, now I couldn't see the way I had come...the bomb bay was black as could be.

Way down in the body of the plane, I could see the spotlight which the fire chief had and I called for him to light my way out and he proceeded to come up towards the cabin a little way. I yelled for that guy with the light to come back and give me a break. Just as I was in this predicament I heard a moan in the little booth they had the radarscope mounted in and I was amazed to find I wasn't alone. I heard feeble groaning come from the telephone booth size office just up on the right-side flight desk. There was a big man, an officer, lying all twisted sideways on the floor of the booth.

I recognized that there was somebody not known to the other flight people who was hurt and immediately called for help to get him out. Then I opened the door and there was an officer, semi-conscious, and the fireman arrived and called for two more hands to take the man down the catwalk as carefully as possible. My assignment then was to cradle the man's head as obviously he had suffered a head injury. At this point, Mr. Flashlight stuck his head back in the bomb bay and I was able to tell him we need a couple of strong boys here to lift the obviously injured member of what I perceived to be part of the original flight crew. Guided by the fireman, two GI's whom I did not know and two firemen, we eased the injured man to the end of the catwalk and then eased him under the catwalk to the ground under the plane. Whereupon he was borne away to medical aid. At least I hope he was. It was the last I heard or saw of him because at that point the M.P. contingent told us to go back where we belonged. Too bad they weren't there when the captain needed them! What the condition of this man was then to this day I do not know but he was hurt.

Following this, the military police pushed all of the men away from the crash site and I, of course, ran back to my work station and started to remove spark plugs. About 11 a.m. the sergeant came out from the operations of the line maintenance and told me I was to go over with two other boys to explain what happened to the Commanding Officer. I spoke to somebody — maybe the first sergeant — and he told me and the other two fellows that we were going to be put in for the soldier's medal. That was the first and last word on that subject that I ever heard. That week the squadron newspaper carried a small account of what happened but it did not resemble what really took place because for one thing, I was the one who turned off the engines and it was only me and the fire chief in the airplane when the injured officer was discovered.

From *The Transmitter*, Wednesday, February 28, 1945:
"Though too modest to discuss their quick action in the emergency, Pfc. Bob Miller, Pfc. Tommy Shuck and Cpl. Bill Murden emerge as the heroes of the week. When two planes collided and caught fire, the three mechanics ran to the scene. Miller crawled into one plane and helped carry out an unconscious lieutenant, assisted by Shuck and Murden."

CHAPTER 7

A Little Corner of England in the Florida Scrub

Drive east in southwest Florida from the sparkling sandy beaches of Naples, Fort Myers and Sarasota. Soon the tourist areas give way to scrub and pasture land. This is cattle country, in the largest beef cattle state east of the Mississippi. This is also a place where highways run to and through small towns, some little changed even as the state has boomed.

One is Arcadia. On its outskirts is a cemetery, little different from those found in such towns.

But if you come here any Memorial Day, you'll see a strange sight. Hundreds of people will be standing around a single row of graves. They will be surrounded by wreaths. Speeches will be made and flowers laid to honor the gallant dead from a great world war. These are not Arcadia boys, or Florida boys, or even American boys. This is a little corner of England. As a bright sun shines overhead, the Union Jack and the Royal Air Force ensign, fluttering in the thick air and light breezes of a Florida summer, are slowly lowered to half-staff. The crowd at Oak Ridge Cemetery sings *God Bless America* and *God Save the Queen*. And, one at a time, twenty-three little Union Jacks, the kind that fit on a tabletop, are jabbed into the ground — one at each grave of British pilots who died a half century ago a long way from home.

A Place to Train

During World War II, as Germany made England a war front, the British desperately needed a place to train their pilots. America set up six flight-training schools. England sent about 2,000 British cadets. About 100 trained at schools in Arcadia and about 80 miles east in Clewiston. The schools were privately contracted to the British government by Dr. John Riddle, who founded an aeronautics college in Daytona Beach.

A total of 952 cadets died nationwide, twenty-three of them at the Arcadia and Clewiston schools. Nineteen of the twenty-three died in air-related incidents, two in auto accidents and two of disease. With England at war, as when its empire spanned the globe, it was often impractical to

53

ship the dead home. So they were buried where they died, and their graves became a little piece of the realm. Arcadia is believed to be one of only six places in America where British soldiers are buried in a special plot. Although this piece of Oak Ridge cemetery was never officially deeded to the British government, it will always be recognized as British soil.

On Memorial Day, people come as they have every year. Some are local residents who came to know the pilots.

"Our little town accepted these young men," Edna Watkins of Arcadia's American Legion Auxiliary said at the 1988 gathering. "Now we come to remember them in honor and love."

Some are British tourists. Some are veterans of the flight schools who timed their holidays to honor their pals on this day. Some are expatriates who moved to Florida from England or from Canada, Australia and other former members of the British Commonwealth, and were bused over from retirement communities on both Florida coasts.

In 1988, Olive Moffett, head of a British group in St. Petersburg, recited a eulogy often spoken in her native land.

"At the going down of the sun and in the morning, we will remember them," she said.

Some are current officers of both the U.S. Air Force and the Royal Air Force, which has a permanent exchange post at MacDill Air Force Base in Tampa.

"All of these men were trained in the pursuit of ideals we in the West still cherish," RAF Group Captain P.G. Johnson, assistant RAF attaché at the British Embassy in Washington, said at the 1988 ceremony. "The lives of these men continue to be remembered in this corner of a foreign country that is forever England."

It Was Crosskey

Those whose hearts hold a place for the British trainees buried in Arcadia show their respect at the annual memorial ceremony. At the 1988 event, each of those given the honor of placing a Union Jack at a grave followed with a moment of reflection or a snappy salute. A man in a Scottish kilt played the lament on a set of bagpipes. Many of those who died were victims of inexperience and Florida's unpredictable weather, said Jim Cousins, one of the American trainers. He recalled the night fog descended on a Clewiston landing field and two planes collided on the ground. He still remembers the cadet who died.

"It was Crosskey," he said. And there in front of him was the marker of

Roger Crosskey, with the notation that he died January 20, 1942.

Brian Mortimore came all the way from Bristol, England. He had made sure the cemetery was a stop on his American holiday. He could still envision the flashing smile of his fellow cadet, Lionel Viggers.

"He was an outgoing fellow who enjoyed himself and liked to do pranks," Mortimore said as he stood before Viggers' grave. He said Viggers died one night—October 4, 1944, according to the grave marker—when a bolt of lightning struck his plane in a storm. Viggers was but a month away from finishing training and was engaged. Mortimore had the painful task of sending the pilot's personal belongings to his family. He said he will always remember this place across the sea "with great affection. It's like coming back to friends. It's all very touching." He said his pal Viggers "couldn't be in better keeping."

Jim Cotte of Winnipeg, then in his mid-40s, hadn't been born when Canada fought with its British brothers in World War II, but he'd come over from the town of Port Charlotte, north of Fort Myers, to pay his respects.

"It's our turn to do some work for the men who fought so we didn't have to," he said.

Hundreds of RAF members still train in America, said Mark Leakey, leader of the squadron of British exchange officers at MacDill Air Force Base. Leakey said these ceremonies will go on every year forever.

"That's why we have Memorial Day, isn't it?" he asked. "We can't forget. We can't afford to forget."

Molly Cox, formerly of Sheffield, England, was one of four women from the Daughters of the British Empire club in Melbourne, Fla.

"These lads were all British, but there were Americans who died too," she said. "They were all some mother's son. I always think that all the lads should be respected. It's always the young lives..."

Oak Ridge Cemetery in Arcadia is open to the public. It is west of town on Wilson Street, north of State Road 70. Arcadia is about 90 miles southwest of Tampa and about 175 miles northwest of Miami. Information on cemetery or Memorial Day ceremony: DeSoto County Chamber of Commerce: (941) 494-4033.

The RAF plot at the Arcadia Cemetery is recognized by a historic marker. (Courtesy of the Florida State Photographic Archives)

CHAPTER 8

An Abominable Situation:
Black Exploitation in the War Effort

With World War II draining the labor force, America's winter vegetable crop needed harvest help. No problem, the Palm Beach County Board of Public Instruction said in 1942. It changed the schedule of black schools, closing them in the winter to make the black students available to work the growers' fields. The board's action, which would be considered an outrage now, was consistent with the times. What is remarkable is that the county's black educators were able then to pressure the board to end the "abominable situation." This victory and another one in the courts over pay were two of Palm Beach County blacks' contributions to the nationwide battle for education equality. A school in West Palm Beach County is now named for U.B. Kinsey, one of several black educators who met the challenge and won.

Unlike most of the South, where black disenfranchisement extended to the school systems, Palm Beach County's black educators had two things going for them—their own school district and their own union. District 9, also called "The Reserve," was believed to be the only independent black school system in the South. The 4,500-student district was supported by black taxpayers and its leaders were elected by blacks. It encompassed only a small area in what is now central West Palm Beach but wielded rare power among the white power structure of the 1940s. Its cornerstone was Industrial High School, which housed as many as 2,000 students, drawing not only from Palm Beach County but also from Martin, which had no black high school.

The board did not dare press its split-term order on District 9 itself, but it did infuriate blacks countywide by doing so for more than twenty small black schools outside District 9. The farmers who owned South Florida's sprawling crops in the Glades and along the coasts had seen their white laborers head off to war. And the supply of Caribbean workers had been reduced by the chaos of World War II. Farmers were desperate for manpower.

Palm Beach County schools superintendent Dr. John I. Leonard reported to his board at a 1942 meeting that he had received a petition from growers in Boynton Beach and had been briefed on "the seriousness of the situation in the Glades area." The trustees had directed Leonard to make "arrangements so the Negro children would be available next year" for harvests. Leonard, acting on information from county agricultural agent Marvin "Red" Mounts about the heaviest harvest times, scheduled the black schools to run June 8 through December 18.

It didn't take long for black educators to react. Kinsey and C. Spencer Pompey recalled confronting Leonard.

"There was no earthly reason schoolchildren should interrupt their future or education to pick crops for people that wanted cheap labor," Kinsey said.

The two sarcastically asked Leonard why black youngsters were being called to aid the war effort by working in the fields while whites were not.

"We just didn't want to be more patriotic than white students," Pompey said.

It took two years for the school board to budge, but it did. A major factor was advice from its chairman, an attorney, that the practice might be violating the law, Pompey recalled. In March 1944, at the height of the war, the board put black schools back on a nine-month term. Though the board gave itself an out for "crop emergencies in which Negro children would be needed for harvesting," it was clear the black educators and their union had won a second victory over the school establishment.

"We met with this abominable situation as we did with the salary question," Kinsey said.

The Salary Question

After white teachers with five years of experience got a $25 raise to $140 a month — about $1,400 a month in 1990s dollars — and similarly qualified blacks didn't, blacks' outrage led to the founding of the Palm Beach County Teachers Association. About 85 percent of the county's 115 black teachers joined; Pompey, principal of Washington Elementary in Riviera Beach, was named president. Charles H. Stebbins Jr., a longtime educator in Palm Beach County, offered his name to top the 1941 federal class-action suit. The lawyer for the plaintiffs was Thurgood Marshall, then attorney for the national Association for the Advancement of Colored People and later a U.S. Supreme Court justice.

The federal judge ruled a year later for the black teachers in Palm Beach County. The victory couldn't help Stebbins; he had been fired and was waiting tables in New York. He never returned to education. He died in

1991. But the ruling did strengthen the association and steeled it for its next battle, the harvesting controversy.

And ironically, while the judge in Stebbins' case cited the Supreme Court's 1896 ruling that public institutions could be separate if they were equal, the teachers' victory marked another step toward the landmark 1954 *Brown vs. Board of Education* decision that outlawed segregation.

The Palm Beach County Teachers Association merged in 1967 with a white teachers group to form the Palm Beach County Classroom Teachers Association. John I. Leonard, who was president of Palm Beach Junior College for a decade, died in July 1961; the high school named for him opened in Lake Worth four years later. C. Spencer Pompey retired in 1979 as principal of Carver Middle School in Delray Beach. He died in July 2001. A park in Delray Beach is named for him. And U.B. Kinsey retired in 1989 as principal of Palmview Elementary School — the old Industrial High where he began his career. It was renamed in 1989 as U.B. Kinsey/Palmview Elementary. Kinsey died in April 2005.

CHAPTER 9

"How Did My Brother Die?"

"MURDERED."

There it was, clearly visible, even though the document was barely legible. Kay Hutchins had found it on page 80 of 129 pages of documents that had shown up one day in her mailbox. After believing for four decades that her brother, Newell Brainard of West Palm Beach, had died when his blazing bomber slammed into a German cow pasture, Hutchins had learned only a few years earlier, and just by accident, that his death might have come differently. It had taken several more months of dogged detective work slogging through the maze of federal archives and a few strokes of good luck before she came across the September 17, 1947, burial report that finally told her the truth.

Her brave brother had not died over Kassel, during one of World War II's most tragic battles, where dozens died in minutes after a navigator's blunder sent them into the teeth of German defenses. He'd survived his crash, only to be interrogated and tortured by war criminals, who finally shot him in the head and dumped his body in a mass grave.

Hutchins still hasn't figured out why the U.S. government had never gotten around to telling her family. Perhaps it was to spare them the awful truth during a time when America wanted to forget the costs of the war and move on. Or just maybe the information became lost in the bureaucracy. And she says she probably would never have found out if not for a chance exchange of letters with an Ohio man who had survived the furious air battle and a German who had watched the carnage over Kassel as a young boy and made its study his life's avocation. It is the friendship that developed between these auxiliary victims of war, once enemies, that may be the only good to come from the murder of Newell Brainard—that and the peace of mind that came with the grim truth, concealed all these years.

And yet Kay Hutchins often wonders if she'd been better off never knowing.

Palm Beach Fly-Boy

Newell White Brainard—"Curly"—earned letters in football, baseball and track before he graduated from Palm Beach High School in 1938. He enrolled in the first-ever class at Palm Beach Junior College, the first junior college in the state. He joined the executive training program at Atlantic National Bank—now Union National Bank—and worked at its main branch in downtown West Palm Beach. He was also part of the "Cowboys of the Sea," a group that helped rescue swimmers off Palm Beach.

As Morrison Field, now Palm Beach International Airport, became a major military base early in World War II, Newell and his brother got the fly-boy bug watching the planes head east for war.

"You saw servicemen everywhere," Kay Hutchins says. "Anyone who wasn't in uniform wanted to go into uniform."

They both signed up in 1942. Newell was made an Army Aviation cadet January 10, 1943, and took pre-flight training at Maxwell Field in Montgomery, Alabama. In August 1943, he was stationed in Seymour, Indiana. There, on August 14, he married the daughter of the Palm Beach County Tax Collector. In June 1944, just after the D-Day invasion of Europe, he went overseas with the 8th U.S. Army Air Force. The "Mighty 8th," based in England, was the largest air contingent in history, its historians say. His wife had returned to Florida, where she moved in with her mother.

"If you want to be up on your air corps slang," Newell wrote his sister Kay in July 1944 from northern Ireland, "if you go on a mission and a 'Jerry' breaks you away from the formation, 'You've had it.' Are you hep?"

During a bombing mission later that month, the *Blasted Event*, a 28-ton, four-engine, long-range B-24 Liberator, took anti-aircraft fire and its instruments were knocked out. The old plane was unable to climb out of high, thick clouds and the crew said later it went into a roll. Footprints were later found on its ceiling. Newell, the co-pilot, and the pilot, Lt. Ray Carrow, were able to wrestle the plane back into control and limp home. Their harrowing ordeal made several newspapers, including the Palm Beach *Times*, so Kay Hutchins clipped the article.

"Eighteen finished and 17 to go," Newell wrote a week later. After 35 missions, pilots got to go home. "I hope I can get these behind me before too long and then maybe I'll be home for Xmas and New Year's Day."

In August, Newell spent his first anniversary an ocean away from his wife. He also had learned his brother was missing in action, shot down July 26.

"At the rate our boys are pushing the 'Jerries' toward the east and the Russians are pushing toward the west it ought not to take very long for them to figure that the 'jig is up for them,'" he wrote September 3. When he wrote on September 26, he had learned his brother was a prisoner of war at Stalag Luft IV—an airmen's prison camp 4 in northeastern Germany.

"Now they've had it," he wrote in September. "We'll go after those S-B's and get Bill back with us...I'll settle for Prisoner-of-War any time. He will be treated all right, I am sure. His food won't be as good and he might not stay as clean but they won't do him any harm. That's no propaganda because no case has been reported of any Americans being maltreated."

His letter was postmarked the next day, September 27—the day he was to fly his 20th, and last, mission. It was the day he would learn his optimistic assessment of German treatment was wrong.

The Skies Over Kassel

On a misty morning, Wednesday, September 27, 1944, the 8th U.S. Army Air Force left bases in England for five targets in central Germany—Cologne, Mainz, Ludwigshafen, Mannheim, and Kassel. The 445th bomber group was assigned to the Henschel locomotive factory in Kassel, which was believed to be building tanks and cannons. At the point where the groups split into separate bombing runs, amid cloudy skies and poor visibility, the leader of the 445th deviated 30 degrees from his route.

"That Mickey man"—the radar navigator—"in the lead ship has screwed up," one navigator said over his intercom. "We shouldn't have turned yet."

In the co-pilot's seat of one plane, about to head into a hornet's nest with his fellow fliers, was Curly Brainard. Within moments of the navigator's error, the planes of the 445th had been separated from the other bombers—and their protective fighter escorts. The bombers of the 445th mistakenly flew to the town of Goettingen and dropped their bombs around several small towns with no casualties or significant damage. Then the lumbering, vulnerable bombers followed the planned route back—fifty miles behind the other planes, which had made a successful raid on Kassel. Veterans say the leader may have actually thought he was still in course and had bombed Kassel.

"It was a complete fiasco," recalls battle veteran George M. Collar.

The Germans, pursuing the main convoy, scrambled ME-109 Messerschmitts designed to distract American fighters and slower, more deadly Focke Wulf 190 storm fighters especially built to pick off bombers. About forty-five miles southeast of Kassel, the 150 German fighters instead came upon the lagging 445th. Within three minutes, twenty-five American bombers were spiraling down in flames. Five more later crashed trying to get home or returned so damaged they were declared total losses. It was the greatest loss of bombers for any individual group of the 8th Air Force.

During the battle, gunners aboard the bombers and several late-arriving American P-51 fighters managed to down several German fighters.

In *Patches*, Newell and pilot Paul Carrow saw the bomber in front of them burst into flames. Newell pounded on Carrow's arm; an engine was afire and Germans were bearing down. The tail assembly of *Patches* had been all but destroyed. A fire spread and the crew was bailing out.

"I nudged Brainard (and) he was out of his seat like a light," Carrow later wrote a companion from a POW camp, Stalag Luft I, along the Baltic in northern Germany. "Brainard was trying to get out (but) the bomb bay was a roaring inferno. I tried to get out of my seat, but I was paralyzed too."

Carrow finally made it to the bomb bay but found only blue sky; the plane had split in two. He had no choice but to leap into the abyss. A German soldier was on him the moment he hit the ground. The soldier's only words were a question: "Jude?(Jew?)"

Carrow, one of 121 Americans taken as prisoners of war that day, knew when he bailed out that Newell was no longer in the plane. Ironically, he moved in the 1960s from Long Island to Miami, not far from where his co-pilot had grown up, and has since corresponded with Kay Hutchins. He is the last survivor of his crew. Carrow had never learned his co-pilot's fate. He believed, as did most, that Newell was one of the 118 Americans killed that day as their planes fell in a twenty-mile circle around a town of about 13,000 called Bad Hersfeld.

On the ground, a 12-year-old boy watched in awe as the explosions formed black clouds and the sky filled with the parachutes of Americans. Walter Hassenpflug and fellow members of the Bad Hersfeld Hitler Youth had scattered into adjoining fields, gathering and burning leaflets and ration cards dropped by the American planes. Two months later, during an American raid, a bomb struck his house, killing his parents. Newell Brainard and Hassenpflug never met. But Curly's death was to become a big part of Walter Hassenpflug's life.

War Crimes

For the Germans, nothing inspired more hate or glee and the opportunity for vengeance than a living, downed American airman. With American GIs fighting Germans far off at the front, it was the U.S. fighters alone who the Germans saw destroying their factories and towns. And it was the airmen alone who people could punish when they fell from the sky.

But the first Germans to encounter Newell Brainard presented only compassion. They found him lying amid his parachute in a field, suffering a head wound, and took him to a nearby village, where a Red Cross nurse treated him.

In the next town, the German government ran an *Ostarbeitslager*, a labor camp where citizens of eastern European countries were forced to mine copper. Its commanders, under orders to pick up any downed American airmen and hold them for military authorities, quickly learned some had been captured nearby.

"They were supposed to detain them," Gunter Lemke, Hassenpflug's interpreter and associate on much of the Kassel battle research, said recently from Germany. "They took it on their own to murder these people."

Local Germans really could do nothing, Lemke says.

"Everywhere you went there was a silent opposition, but nobody could never dare to say that openly," he says. "The government was spying on everybody. That's how these regimes existed. If anybody said one wrong word against the government he was gone. That's how they kept strict control over the people."

The first pilot to die had the misfortune of parachuting in front of the home of a German soldier on leave. A camp commander who happened to be driving by ordered the soldier to shoot the man. Two other pilots were also captured. After a failed escape attempt they, too were taken to the camp. And they, too, were shot. Later in the day, someone called to the camp. There were two more Americans to pick up. One was Newell Brainard. At the labor camp, the fliers were interrogated and beaten. Finally, they were led outside and shot with pistols. Then all five were thrown into a single grave in the town cemetery.

Killed in Action

Back in West Palm Beach, the Brainard family learned Newell was missing in action. It had been just a few months since they got the same word on brother Bill. Newell Brainard and his sister, Kay, had been born sixteen months apart, two of four children of Alice White Brainard. Their father died when they were young.

In November 1944, Kay—who had been secretary to the commander at The Breakers hotel in Palm Beach, which had been converted to the Ream military hospital—joined the American Red Cross and went to Europe. By Christmas she had learned Bill was alive, a POW. As the Russians and Americans joined to crush the Nazis, Bill and others went on a forced march through Germany. He eventually was freed and reunited with Kay in England. But there was still no word about Newell.

"You have my heartfelt sympathy in your sorrow and it is my earnest hope that the fortitude which has sustained you in the past will continue through this distressing period of uncertainty," Maj. Gen. J.A. Ulio wrote Newell's wife on May 7, 1945.

After the war, Kay went to occupied Germany — first to Aschaffenburg, a rail center near Frankfurt that was all but destroyed by American bombing raids and where she met some of the first GIs returning from the horrors at Dachau. She later went to Erlangen, only a few miles from Nuremburg, and attended some of the infamous war crime trials.

Being around Germans, "I soon learned that they were much like all of us — doing what had to be done in wartime — and I was able to handle my hatred and resentment," she wrote years later.

In September 1945, after he had been missing one year, the Army declared Newell KIA — Killed In Action. The Brainard family had placed two blue stars in their window for Newell and Bill but, because of Newell's uncertain status, one was never replaced with a gold star indicating a death in war. The family never held a memorial ceremony.

A September 1947 report identified Newell. He had been buried in March 1946 at the American military cemetery at St. Avold, France, as unknown soldier X-1535. His body was later disinterred in a highly decomposed state and the military used dental records, physical characteristics and the name "Brainard" found on a wool undershirt on the body to identify him. It wasn't until April 1948, a delay about which Kay is still bitter, that the American military informed the family Newell Brainard's body had been positively identified. It gave no indication the cause of death was any different from that earlier given: shot down over Germany. Newell's mother opted to have him remain buried with his comrades. His widow remarried. His mother died in 1957, never knowing how her son really died.

Justice

Even as the atrocities were taking place near Kassel, the labor camp's days were numbered. That week the Russians were in the Baltics, Bulgaria and Yugoslavia; the Allies were marching through the Netherlands. Within months, the war was over, the Reich destroyed. Soon after setting up an occupation force, Americans began asking residents about any downed airmen. The townspeople led them to the mass grave containing the bodies of the Americans.

A February 28, 1945, report on Newell's as-yet unidentified body said he had been clubbed, then shot. According to reports, the remains had been found in a mattress cover in a box, two bullet holes in his head.

Residents identified suspects. Seven were rounded up; an eighth had committed suicide on the last day of the war. The Americans set up a war crimes trial that began June 3, 1947, in the town of Dachau, site of the notorious concentration camp. Local residents testified against the mine bosses. One said in his defense that one of the Americans had attacked him and another German. On February 5, 1948, the military court ruled all but one of the seven defendants "were eager principals in the beatings or killings and not merely curious bystanders, as each accused contended he was." Three were hanged, one was sentenced to death but had already been hanged for another crime, and the other three were given jail terms. The camp commanders would have shared all Germans' hatred for airmen, and most were put in such jobs specifically because they were fanatics and were especially cruel, Hassenpflug and Lemke say. But it would be pure speculation to try to place a firm motive on the slayings, the two say. Kay Hutchins said her brother's murderers "were just mean, I think."

A Letter From Germany

The drama of the Kassel battle intrigued Walter Hassenpflug in later years, especially when veterans from both sides began visiting the area. He began gathering everything he could on it—interviewing townspeople and contacting veterans groups and archives from both countries. His efforts intensified in the 1980s with the launching of a project to build a battle memorial.

In later years, Kay became an assistant to actor and part-time Palm Beach resident Douglas Fairbanks Jr. In the early 1980s, she was a volunteer historian for the part of the 8th Air Force Bomb Group to which she'd been attached in her Red Cross years. It was through that group's newsletter that the chain of events began which revealed the truth about Newell Brainard's death. In April 1987, Kay Hutchins got a letter from Kassel veteran George Collar in Tiffin, Ohio, who had seen in the air group's newsletter a note from her asking for details of her brother's death. Collar attached a copy of a March 1987 letter to him from Walter Hassenpflug in Germany. He had been seeking Collar's help in researching the battle. Kay's gaze scanned to the bottom of the letter and leaped to the mention of her brother's name. "I do not know where and how Newell W. Brainard died," Hassenpflug wrote. "It is possible that he landed with his chute near the village of Nentershausen and was one of the five airmen who were shot to death there."

"I was horrified," Kay says now. "I owed it to myself to find out."

"Your mention of the five officers being 'shot' was the first I've ever heard of this possibility," Hutchins wrote Hassenpflug in April 1987. "I can't help wondering if the War Department knew and purposely kept the information from my mother and his wife, in an effort not to make matters any more tragic than they already were."

At first, Kay did not tell her brother or sister about this startling new conjecture. Hassenpflug had the names of three of the five slain airmen but couldn't place the other two. He knew Newell might be one. Hassenpflug couldn't piece together the jigsaw puzzle in Germany, so he wrote several letters to the National Archives, but the $700 cost for copies of documents was prohibitive. On February 29, 1988, Hutchins wrote the National Personnel Records Center in search of information.

"It is very strange that the authorities would know who to punish for these murders, and yet not know the names of all of those airmen who suffered this unkind fate," she wrote.

In March 1990, Kay was in New York working with Fairbanks. She decided to board a train for the National Archives military records center near Washington. After spending an entire day in the 8th Air Force files, she was unable to find the report about the Kassel mission. A researcher told her it had been missing since 1970. As a dejected Kay prepared to leave, the researcher stopped her. He told her what she really wanted was her brother's burial file. He would dig it up and send her copies. About a month later, 129 pages arrived.

"Nobody had ever looked past the first page of his file," she says now. "It wasn't until I reached page 80 that the story began to jell."

The September 17, 1947, burial report—the one with which the Army had so long ago identified Newell Brainard as the body that had been discovered in a mass grave—was a poor copy, but one word on it could clearly be read:

"Murdered."

Still Missing

It had taken four years for Newell Brainard's status to change from "MIA" to "KIA." The families of many World War II soldiers are still waiting. While the plight of the estimated 3,000 soldiers missing in action in Vietnam has sparked national interest and a string of films ranging from the provocative to the exploitive, families across the United States still wonder about the estimated 78,750 MIAs from World War II and about

8,200 from Korea.

Because of the fierce fighting in two different war theaters, both the military and families agree all but a handful of the World War II MIAs died in action and their bodies were never recovered. But some officials have theorized up to 20,000 American POWS were taken from German prison camps to the Soviet Union at the end of World War II.

In 1992, previously secret Soviet files showed at least 70 American POWS were taken. But Russian officials said all but four escaped, and they were trying to determine the fate of those four.

Meanwhile, a retired colonel and prominent historian and senior defense adviser to Russian President Boris Yeltsin has told American officials a small number of American POWs were sent to gulags—prison camps. Those with Russian sounding surnames or knowledge of the language were accused of spying and sentenced to 25-year terms in the labor camps. Others were charged with siding with Nazis to fight Russians. At the first meeting of a joint U.S.-Russian commission, Russian officials turned over the names of eight Americans who had died in Soviet gulags. But they said the eight were American citizens who had fought in the German army.

A Marker in the Forest

"It now appears," George Collar wrote Hutchins in June 1990, "that your fears as to Newell's fate have now been confirmed. However, you and your brother can now console yourselves with the idea that at least you know what happened, which is better than never knowing at all."

And Hassenpflug wrote in sketchy English, "With great sympathy I learned about fate your family suffered. I am sorry for bringing back to your memory those painful events because of my research."

There's no way to know after all these years why or how the military never told Newell's family the circumstances of his death, says Doug Howard, mortuary programs specialist for the U.S. Army. Howard notes the military did not have the communications setup it does now but says it would be pure speculation to blame the omission on bureaucracy. He says there's no evidence the military had a policy of withholding such details from families.

Kay Hutchins knows his killers paid for their crimes. She also knows atrocities were committed on both sides. An American soldier admitted to her machine-gunning five German prisoners because one called him a swine.

On August 1, 1990, Kay and nearly 80 other Americans traveled to a

4,000-foot clearing deep in the Hesse State Forest in central Germany. There, the German people had assembled three granite stones, on which markers detailed the battle of Kassel and listed the 25 German and 118 American airmen who died. The monument had been created in Germany and paid for by thousands of dollars in donations from Americans. Five hundred Germans joined the Americans for a solemn ceremony. As a German Air Force trumpeter played taps, former enemies shook hands. Prayers were offered. Kay finally met Walter Hassenpflug. Through an interpreter, the two shared the stories of how each had lost loved ones to war.

The following day, as church bells tolled, Kay Hutchins would see where her brother's plane crashed and where he parachuted down and the house where a Red Cross nurse had performed an act of mercy later fouled by an act of evil. But for a moment, there in front of the stark stones, she reached out to touch the brass plate and run her finger over her brother's name.

The Tragedy at Kassel: September 27, 1944

1. 8th Air Force leaves bases in England.
2. Planes cross into Germany.
3. 445th bomber group deviates from main convoy.
4. Main convoy bombs planned targets in Kassel.
5. 445th bombs Goettingen; returns via original route.
6. 150 German fighters attack 445th in and around Bad Hersfeld; 25 of 35 bombers shot down. Five more crash en route to base or return so damaged they are declared total losses. American fighters and bomber gunners down 29 German planes. One U.S. fighter downed. Total casualties: 60 airplanes downed; 118 Americans and 25 Germans killed; 121 Americans taken as POWs.
7. Newell Brainard's plane shot down. He parachutes down over Iba and is captured and taken to Suess.
8. Brainard taken to Nentershausen labor camp. He is interrogated, beaten and shot.
9. Brainard's body later moved to U.S. military cemetery in France.
10. War criminals tried at Dachau and hanged or jailed.

THE TOLL:

United States:

2nd division, 445th bomber group: 35 bombers. They were part of the

U.S. Army 8th Air Force's three bomber divisions, comprising 1,092 bombers and 640 escort fighters.

Losses:

25 bombers shot down, 5 crashed or fatally damaged returning home, 4 safely returned to base. One U.S. fighter downed.

118 airmen killed

121 taken Prisoner of War

Germany:

150 ME-109 Messerschmitts and Focke Wulf 190 fighter planes.

Losses:

29 fighters shot down

18 pilots killed; seven Germans killed on ground.

Newell Brainard was captured and murdered after he was shot down. (Photo courtesy of Kay Hutchins)

CHAPTER 10

Shooting Stars and Friendly Fire

Little Davie Cosson never had a chance.

On August 11, 1944, the Army Air Corps dropped four bombs on his uncle's Panhandle farm. His father, uncle and two cousins were killed, and he was paralyzed. It may have been the only time in World War II when civilians in America were killed by "friendly fire." No one can say for sure. There was an investigation, but no one told Cosson its results.

"No inquiry. No interview. Nothing," Isaac David Cosson said in a 1994 interview. He died in January 1999. In the interview, he leans forward in his wheelchair from the porch of his modest Central Florida home. After more than 100 operations, only a stub of a left leg remains below his hip.

"They never did admit it was their fault," he says, his eyes narrowing. "No one apologized. Son, they pushed it under the rug."

Who knows how many times Cosson has recounted that horrific night in the last 50 years? He recites the ghastly details almost in rote, "like I'm telling it about somebody else." But ask if he's been able to exorcise or even dull those images and you throw off his stride. He stops. Tears well.

"You can't express it," he says after a moment. "It's terrible. You don't ever get over it. I don't. I live with it every day."

Nowhere to Run

The Cossons were simple country folk. Three different families ran modest farms, raising mostly turkey, along the same road in the Alaqua community, southwest of De Funiak Springs. Four cousins were off at war serving their country. Every Friday afternoon, the families would gather at one of their homes. This night was at Uncle Jim's place. The clan would take part in what has become almost a lost art: sitting on the front porch talking as the sun set late on a midsummer night. David and his cousins, 13-year-old Jim Jr. ("Bubby") and 15-year-old Winnie Lee were packing the *Grit* family newspapers they sold for pocket money.

About a half-mile away lay the eastern edge of the Eglin Army Air Field reservation, a 725-square mile sprawl across three Panhandle counties; it is the largest installation in what was until recently called "the free world." With the war heating up in those first weeks after D-Day, Eglin was making night bombing runs, using live bombs. The Cossons always knew when the bombs were coming; planes would drop location flares on parachutes that almost recreated daylight.

"They'd light the whole sky, the ground," Cosson recalls. "It was like you could pick up the head of a pin."

A cluster bomb has the effect of a sackful of hand grenades landing and exploding simultaneously. Hot metal scatters in a killing spray. The bomb is designed for maximum casualties. David's father, Alfred, had written Eglin, worried that bombs fell so close to his home.

"They said there was no danger whatsoever," his son says bitterly.

Power hadn't yet been run to those rural areas, so by about 9 p.m. that night in August 1944, as people were saying their goodbyes, the darkness swallowed them, bothered only by a feeble kerosene lamp on the Cosson porch. Alfred Cosson saw four shooting stars. He told David, "that's a bad sign."

Flares began to light the sky.

"Then we heard those planes coming across the fields," David says, beginning the story he has told so many times.

Suddenly everyone could hear the unmistakable whistle. Incoming.

"They just grabbed each other by the hand and started running."

But the Cossons had nowhere to run.

"Just Screaming and Hollering and Moaning and Dying."

"Bubby was standing in the door on the porch. He said, 'Daddy, c'mon!' It hit Bubby between the eyes, just like it hit him with a meat cleaver. The impact was so hard it knocked his brains to a window. He crumbled down on the floor in a pool of blood."

"Uncle Jim started to go in on a porch. A piece hit him in the back of the head, spun him around three times. Each time blood splattered on the porch. I was right behind him (Uncle Jim). I didn't know where to run. A piece hit me in the head (and) knocked me to my knees. I made about three steps. A piece hit me in the back; knocked me down. I was paralyzed. The impact was so hard it knocked the feeling out. As I lay on the ground, another bomb fell 3-1/2 feet away. The impact was so powerful it knocked me 3 to 4 feet in the air."

"Frank (David's 10-year-old cousin) was going through the gate. He got hit in the stomach. It knocked him to his knees. When he got up he was holding his guts in with his hands. As he walked in the house he was calling his momma and crying. He fell on the porch and passed out."

"Dad had Winnie by the hand. They were running. The bomb fell right between them. The impact knocked the soles off his shoes. Broke every bone in his body. They had to roll him in a sheet to pick him up. Winnie's left leg was jerking. She was moaning. The back of her head was matted with blood. Lord. She didn't have a face. Her face was completely blowed off. No eyes or nothing. Just blood..."

"Thomas, the baby, (David's cousin) had one piece of steel in his hip. He was 4 years old. A bomb cut the head of the bed off. It was a steel bed. Aunt Bell (Uncle Jim's wife, Annabelle) was running out and screaming."

"She had a big gash in her right leg. Mother was hit under the arm. She had a hole as big as your two fists. It happened in a matter of minutes. I could see Bubby lying in a pool of blood. Noisy? Oh, Lord, yes. The powder was so thick you couldn't hardly breathe. Nobody said anything. Just screaming and hollering and moaning and dying. That's all you could hear.'"

A Cascade of Blood

Uncle Jim, his son, Bubby, and daughter, Winnie Lee, and his brother Alfred, David's father, were killed that night. The others lay badly hurt. David's cousin, Wallace Cosson, 15, had stepped on the back porch of his home, just 250 yards to the north, when he saw the flares come down.

"The bombs started a quarter-mile from the house and went right through the house in a line," Wallace recalls. "It was like a machine gun."

Shirtless and barefoot, he raced down the road into blinding smoke, screams and death. He turned, ran back home, and got his pickup. Wallace loaded the broken bodies in the back of the truck and headed for De Funiak Springs, about 7 miles of dirt roads away.

"He picked me up like I was a baby," David says. "I could see my Dad laying over there with his mouth open, eyes open."

Winnie's mangled head was laid on his chest and he held her hand the whole way. Wallace pulled up to the small Lakeside Clinic, jumped out and dropped the tailgate. Blood cascaded down. One nurse looked into the pickup and said, "Take them to the funeral home." Just then an officer from Eglin showed up. He said, "'If you don't take those people in, I'll take over this hospital by martial law,'" David recalls.

Soon military vehicles were driving the victims to the Eglin hospital, 29 miles away. Wallace Cosson, who'd been only reacting, not thinking, finally had a moment to absorb what he'd seen in the smoke.

"I got sick to my stomach. I had blood all over me."

What Happened?

Inquiries by the Palm Beach *Post* of more than a dozen federal agencies and archives came up with a few documents summarizing the accident and its grisly results. None said how it happened. It's not likely the report was buried, rather that it was simply misfiled some time in the past five decades, archivists say. The only official word had been given to newspapers just after the bombing:

"Some of the bombs hit within the target area. However, for some undetermined reason, a number of the bombs failed to release at the proper point and were released about one-half mile from the edge of the reservation."

"It is believed at this time that the cause of the accident was the failure of a mechanical device for the releasing of the bombs and that several bombs hung on the device after the release had been made, thereby carrying the bombs beyond the target and finally releasing near the property of the victims resulting in severe damage."

The bomb release worked on simple gravity. The doors opened and the bombs started to slide out, but for some reason they caught. After the plane had crossed the base boundaries in the darkness, it made a big turn, and the angle became sharp enough to dislodge the bombs.

Immediately after the attack, the four Cosson sons who were in the military pressed for information. At one point, a colonel sat down with Shelley Cosson, David's brother, and told him as much as he could.

"I would have liked to have had more of a report," Shelley says now. He says he got too busy getting on with his life and that of his shattered family to continue his chase. And he says he understands how the accident could have occurred.

"We didn't have the pilots and they were training these pilots really too fast and the guys were just doing the best they could," he says.

The Cossons said they wanted to talk to the pilot. They said his supervisors had told him of the accident and transferred him. He says if the pilot was much of a man, he'd have tried to contact David over the years. A nurse had told him the pilot had suffered a nervous breakdown and been institutionalized. No one will say for sure.

"It was carelessness," David Cosson says now. "The kid was doing his job. If he wasn't well-trained enough to be in that plane, it wasn't his fault. Naturally the government tried to cover it up. I'm still resentful. They didn't care about me. They didn't care about the rest of them."

Sent Home to Die

The Cosson family had no life or health insurance. Cosson's mother --
she and the others recovered — was awarded $259 to cover the accumu-
lated and anticipated medical costs of young David. The nurses called him
"Davie," and the doctors gave him a few months to live. Complications set
in — anemia, infection, gangrene. Toes came off in the shower. His right leg
was removed. So was his bladder. Time and again they sent him home,
believing nothing more could be done. He lived, off and on, at Eglin hospital, for more than a decade.

In 1946, the 79th Congress passed a bill that gave $30,000 to the Cosson
family, including $6,000 for young David. Payments for the dead had been
cut from $10,000 to $5,000 after acting Secretary of War Robert P. Patterson
called them "excessive." When the government paid Alfred Cosson's
estate, it deducted the balance of his farm loan — $836 — minus 3 1/2 per-
cent interest for the three years since his death. The 81st Congress gave
David another $15,000, but the government never turned it over when a
county judge feared it would dry up too quickly.

David moved to Clermont, a small town about 25 miles west of Orlando,
and paid $3,500 for the modest home where he still lives. He bought a car
with a hand control. In 1953, he was offered a $15,000 settlement — $3,000
of it for the lawyers. He had to sign a release form.

"The man from the federal government said if I didn't sign it I wouldn't
get nothing."

He was twenty-one. He signed. Disabled, in and out of hospitals, his
education ended in the sixth-grade by the attack, he did odd jobs and went
through the nest egg. When it ran out, he went on welfare. He married in
1959. Later his wife, Jimmie Nadine, began doing laundry on the side for
$50 a week. The government reduced his monthly stipend of about $200
because of the income and demanded back income. David had had
enough.

Equitable Considerations

By the mid 1970s, David and his nephew, Robert Mickler, were calling
reporters in northern and central Florida, hoping publicity would push
the government to do right by David. (The two later had a falling out over
royalties for a possible book, and Mickler himself became bedridden by
disease.) After a story ran in the tabloid *National Enquirer*, letters came in
from across the country. Some of the eloquent pleas were from the nurses
who had fawned over little Davie.

Rep. Bob Sikes, D-Crestview, whose district included De Funiak Springs and who had helped push through the original payment just after the accident, began working for more. When Sikes was forced into retirement by scandal in 1979, his replacement, Earl Hutto, D-Pensacola, picked up the fight, asking Cosson be paid the same as veterans with similar injuries.

"It wasn't right for the government to kill and maim these people, although it was accidental, and not compensate them for it," Hutto recalled later.

Assistant Army Secretary Alan J. Gibbs told the Judiciary Committee that, while the time limit for any claim had long since passed, "settlements and legal principles involved in this matter are quashed by the equitable considerations involved." The bill, he said, would lift Cosson "from the poverty existence in which he was placed for the rest of his life." On July 2, 1980, President Jimmy Carter signed a bill that provided Cosson $18,000 a year — more as the cost of living rises — for the rest of his life.

Until his death, Cosson went up every summer to his family property for a big reunion.

Standing in front of his uncle's home is a marker. It lists the names of the dead.

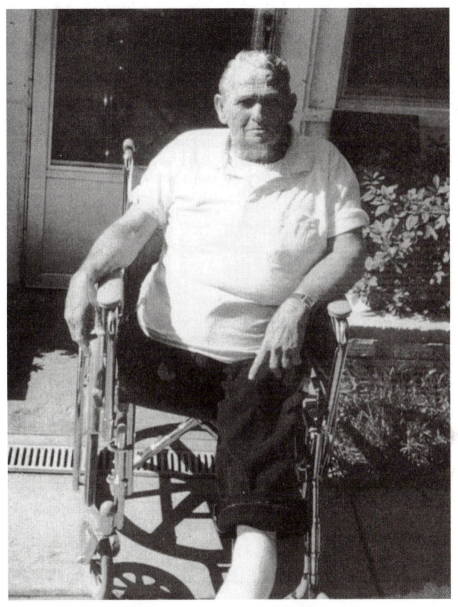

David Cosson outside his Clermont home today.
(Photo courtesy of Eliot Kleinberg)

CHAPTER 11

The Day They Bombed Frostproof

From the air, the pattern of streetlights in this small Central Florida town bore an uncanny resemblance to night bombing markers at nearby Avon Park Bombing Range. So residents shouldn't have been surprised when errant bombs crashed down early on August 22, 1944, and again two nights later. At least five fell that first night, at least two the other night.

Virginia Lyles, worn out from dances at Avon Park, slept through both attacks in a two-story house near downtown.

"After the first one," she recalls now, "I said to a soldier, 'What do you mean bombing us?' He said, 'We're going to do it again' — jokingly. By gosh, they did — the very next night." Lyles died in July 1997.

Dr. Kenneth Dunham was in his office about 1:30 a.m. August 22 when the 100 lb. Bombs — four pounds of explosive and the rest sand, to give just enough of a flash for navigators to see — hurtled down.

"I wondered what the hell was happening," he said. "One of them lit right in the shuffleboard court. That was across the damn road from me. I still didn't know what it was."

The bombs, dropped from 30,000 feet, missed their mistaken target by only 100 feet, Dunham said.

"Damn good shot, I'd say," he said.

Bombs landed in backyards and parking lots and one just missed the bandstand. Mayor John Maxcy found a two-foot hole and twisted metal that "looked like an old street lamp," he told the town newspaper. Two bushels of avocados had been knocked off a tree.

Officials said four bombers from Tampa's MacDill Air Force Base and six from Avon Park had been over the area.

Two nights later, Dunham and another man watched more bombs come down about 12:30 a.m.

"I said, 'That's a hell of a sound.' He says, 'A bomb.' I said, 'Hell. You're crazy.'"

The two raced the three blocks to where Jake Bodow lived in the back of his shoe repair shop. As Bodow had sat at a table reading a newspaper, the bomb had torn through the ceiling, through the floorboards and into the ground, then exploded, Dunham said.

"It went off sticking in the ground and filled that room slap full of smoke," Dunham said. "I couldn't see my hand in front of my face."

"I called in three or four times before I could get the old man up," he said. "He was fumbling around. He had just gotten out of the chair. That damn bomb had come down the back of the chair. Just barely missed."

Mrs. Bodow hadn't been as lucky; the blast had missed the bed by only a few feet, throwing the invalid to the floor. The two rescuers got the Bodows out and called the Avon Park base. Officials there didn't believe them. They finally came out, took a look—another bomb had fallen that night a few blocks away—and said they'd change their patterns so this wouldn't happen again.

No one can find a report on the Frostproof incidents from among the 30,000 air mishaps during World War II. There's no record of whether the Bodows were repaid by the government for damages.

"People didn't sue back then like they do now," Virginia Lyles said.

Virginia Lyles in front of her Frostproof home where she slept through two different bombings runs over the town. (Photo courtesy of Eliot Kleinberg)

CHAPTER 12

A Meeting at Cap's Place

"The Broward County Press had the biggest story in its history nestled right in its midst and couldn't print a word," Miami *Herald* columnist Philip Weidling wrote on June 29, 1961. "It was the day, a few months before the United States entered World War II, when Winston Churchill visited Franklin D. Roosevelt." For four days, the column goes on, the two leaders of the free world secretly met in South Florida.

Too bad it didn't happen.

The dramatic tale of the secret meetings has gotten a lot of mileage in 50 years. It's a highlight of the colorful history of Cap's Place, the popular tavern in Lighthouse Point—near Pompano Beach—where the two leaders allegedly supped. But archivists and scholars of both Roosevelt and Churchill, contacted for this book, insist the meetings never took place. As with most stories, there's some truth to this legend. Scholars say most or all of the leaders said to have visited South Florida, and Cap's, really did—just not all at once. While the *Herald* column says the secret meeting was in January 1941, Cap's owners and historians hired by them to research the restaurant's past say January 1942. The latter is correct, but only for Churchill, scholars say. They can account for his and FDR' movements both times, and say they were never elbow-to-elbow at Cap's tap.

Cap's Place

The story is not the only told around the funky surroundings of Cap's, founded in 1928 by Captain Eugene Theodore Knight. The Cape Canaveral native, son of the Cape's lighthouse keeper, kept busy during Prohibition, running rum from Bimini to Hillsboro Inlet, and finally settled down and set up his tavern. Knight died in 1964 at age 93.

The *Herald* column says Churchill and FDR stayed in January 1941 at the Pompano Beach home (It's actually in adjacent Hillsboro Beach) of Mrs. L.C. Campbell, a relative of Secretary of State Edward R. Stettinus. Along with them, it says, were no less notable a party than General George C. Marshall and Edward, the Duke of Windsor.

The column says the two leaders made frequent trips to the bar, then called "Cappy Knight's Place" and, as now, accessible only by boat, and spent much of their time looking out a picture window toward the Atlantic Ocean. "We imagine that Churchill may well have been rehearsing in his mind a speech he was soon to make in which he offered his people 'blood sweat and tears,' and (said) `we will fight them on the beaches,'" Weidling goes on. He says the Duke may have been thinking about the throne he gave up "for the woman I love." (The Duke abdicated as King of England in 1936 to marry a divorced American). He suggests Marshall, already knowing war was inevitable, may have been wondering how to get troops across that ocean, and FDR may have been thinking of the multitude of young men he'd soon be sending to battle, many of them to their deaths.

The column goes on to say that patrols disguised as fishing boats guarded the beachfront home and agents armed with machine guns gruffly ordered reporters away; it says wire services sent out a bulletin saying no newspaper was to transmit any story about Churchill's whereabouts. It quotes Knight as saying Churchill and Roosevelt were "gay and jaunty" and Marshall liked to relax by dangling his bare feet in the water, but that the Duke was "grave and thoughtful." Nevertheless, Knight says, "They all seemed to have a good time."

In a 1989 proposal that earned Cap's a spot on the National Register of Historic Places, and in a 1990 article for the Historical Association of South Florida, researchers from Coral Springs-based Research Atlantica said the secret meeting took place not in January 1941, but exactly a year later.

Their paper says the leaders held their secret war conferences at Stettinus' villa in Hillsboro Beach along with Marshall, Admiral William "Bull" Halsey and British military leader Lord Beaverbrook. Cap catered several meals and the group had to walk only a short distance to the landing where a boat ferried customers to Cap's. One tale, quoted in a newspaper story years later, quotes Stettinus as saying Knight "can keep his mouth shut in seven languages."

The historical article written for Cap's says that "On one occasion Churchill and Roosevelt dined at Cap's Place." It says the restaurant coordinated getting Roosevelt's wheelchair into the boat and Cap himself served the two.

"No doubt Cap offered Roosevelt and Churchill a refreshing change from the stress of a world at war," the article says.

And it quotes a 1984 Boca Raton *News* story and a 1970 story in *The Boston Globe* in which Cap's chef, Sylvester Love—who has since died—

remembers Churchill and Roosevelt talking to him as he prepared hearts of palm salad.

The Scholars Weigh In

"Alas, I believe Roosevelt did not visit Churchill at Pompano or Palm Beach, though it is a pleasant local fiction," Martin Gilbert, author of *Churchill: A Life*, wrote for this article.

Diaries by both Roosevelt and his associates show he gave an address to Congress on January 6, 1942, then traveled to his home in Hyde Park the next day, returning to Washington on January 11. He never went to Florida that month.

Churchill, worn out by his nation's crisis and under the weather, flew from Washington to Florida January 6 for five days. (Gilbert writes in *Churchill: A Life* that it was January 5; others January 4, but Churchill's autobiography says January 6.)

"Am resting in the South on (medical adviser) Charles Wilson's advice for a few days after rather a strenuous time," Churchill telegraphed to England's Lord Privy on January 7. "President is stopping all mention in the United States press. Please make sure no notice is issued in England, otherwise American press will be vexed, and I shall be overrun with them and tourists."

Churchill wrote in his autobiography that Marshall flew down with him and that he spent the five days "lying about in the shade or the sun, bathing in the pleasant waves, in spite of the appearance on one occasion of quite a large shark. They said it was only a 'ground shark;' but I was not wholly reassured. It is bad to be eaten by a ground shark as by any other."

How ironic it would have been for the leader of England to survive Hitler only to become a meal for a fish. He reportedly told one of his guards that "My bulk has frightened him into deeper water.'"

Wilson, the medical adviser, later noted that Florida's weather "is balmy after the bitter cold of Ottawa," where Churchill had on December 30 delivered to Canada's Parliament his wry response to the challenge that England's neck would be wrung like a chicken: "Some chicken. Some neck." Wilson continued, "Oranges and pineapples grow here. And the blue ocean is so warm that Winston basks half-submerged in the water like a hippopotamus in a swamp." And he wrote home that "The story was put out about that a Mr. Lobb, an invalid requiring quiet, was staying in the house, and to explain my untransatlantic accents when answering the phone, I was his English butler."

The locals weren't fooled, Churchill wrote. "Numbers of people greeted me in Florida, and many pressmen and photographers with whom I had pleasant interchanges, waited outside the (villa)," he wrote. But the news blackout held. During his stay, couriers flew down with papers and telegrams, and Churchill made frequent calls to his people in Washington over the growing world crisis, which now included the United States.

In the early hours of January 12, Churchill left by train for Washington. He flew on January 14 to Bermuda.

By the way, Churchill didn't, as the *Herald* column says, envision his famous "blood, tears, toil and sweat" and "fight on the beaches" speeches during his South Florida visit, either in January 1941 or January 1942. He had already given both speeches — in 1940.

President Franklin Delano Roosevelt and British Prime Minister Winston Churchill meet in Casablanca in 1943. They never met in Florida. (Photo courtesy of *Acme Newspictures* and the Palm Beach *Post*)

CHAPTER 13

A Little Too Close to Home

A certain tension has always existed between the haves and have-nots in time of war. That friction was no different during World War II, where some people were able to wrangle out of serving, earning the contempt of others.

This message to readers appeared on January 2, 1945, on the front page of the Palm Beach *Post*. The article below it had appeared the previous day, New Year's Day.

D.L. Whitehurst could not be found; he may well be long dead.

The bitter article by Whitehurst that ran New Year's Day betrays the feeling by many that America's rich were not equally bearing the burden of war. The apology that follows might seem to bolster the opinion that those of nobility were sacred cows that institutions such as the *Post* and its evening paper, the Palm Beach *Evening Times*, dared not criticize. Others might agree with the management of the *Post* that the front pages of the newspaper were not the proper forums for such commentary. Mr. Whitehurst's criticism is powerful nevertheless.

An Explanation

Yesterday morning there appeared in this space a bitter rasping description of the Palm Beaches starting the New Year which caused probably more amazement to editors and other officials of the *Post-Times* than to readers.

We regret the necessity of publicly repudiating it, but we want all readers to know that it did not, does not and will not represent the feeling of those who are in charge of operating these newspapers.

These newspapers KNOW what the Palm Beaches have done to help the war effort. We know also of the sons who have given their lives in the war. We feel certain that there has been in these communities less than average complacency about the war and its sacrifices.

These communities turned their efforts to war December 7, 1941, and have kept them there since. They will continue to keep them there.

The article under discussion was written by Mr. D.L. Whitehurst, then an assistant on the copy desk, which has charge of selecting the news for the next day's paper. Once weekly, in order to give the head of the copy desk the customary night off, he had immediate charge of the copy desk and therefore had charge of the selection of news material for the following day's paper.

Mr. Whitehurst took advantage of this trust to put into type material extremely distasteful to the editors and other officials of these newspapers. He wrote an editorial and put it on Page 1 in the guise of a news article. It is standard newspaper practice that all editorials must clear with the editor-in-chief, or in his absence from the city, someone designated by him. This editorial by Mr. Whitehurst was not cleared with anyone whomever, and never would have reached print if it had been cleared.

Naturally, Mr. Whitehurst does not continue to work here.

The *Post-Times* regrets publication of the item thoroughly. Even though it reached print in violation of the editors' desires and in violation of ordinary newspaper practice and ethics and, therefore, was not a fault of the *Post-Times* itself, our regret is enormous.

We know what the Palm Beaches have done for the war effort and what their contribution has been. But we will never take advantage of a community which has been faithful — as advantage has been taken of us by one in whom our faith was unjustified.

Palm Beaches Toast New Year
Remembering This Nation At War
By D.L. WHITEHURST
Post Copy Desk

Down at the foot of Clematis, where Flagler Park splits the traffic and spearheads it off toward the sewer-smelly waters of Lake Worth, is where this New Year's story gets its locale.

There, shaded by day by giant palms and winked at by night by traffic lights, stands the honor rolls of those who have gone and will return, and those who have gone and will never come back — save when the salty mists of memory run.

Last night, washed by the light of a tropical moon and flowing red and green in turn under the rays of signal lights the honor table, from a block away, looked like a silent cenotaph. It seemed to guard for those who will never return something akin to honor, hold for those who may get back something significant to the past and to those who never left a message reproachful to the present and sacred to that which must mold a national spirit for the future.

In the flickering shades of night that mixed man-made lights with those of nature's moon the hundreds of names on the honor roll looked like black-draped windows in a deserted castle. Like the tides of time humanity flowered unchecked past this silent symbol of American patriotism.

It was New Year's Eve. This nation is at war.

A couple of blocks away, either to the right or the left, revelers drank to the New Year. Far down the lanes of an uncertain future they saw brighter days, even if they could not make out the hands on their own wristwatches. Half drunk women heard their drunker men tell why this bloody mess so far, far away would be over before another New Year shall dawn.

Thanks to the Yanks in the tanks!

And so last night did that part of Americanism which is so ready to fight a war that knows no mud, no gaping, oozing wounds, no dying buddies, no fear of death that often turns to hope, celebrate the coming of the New Year.

Raw whiskey does not smell good, even when mixed with a woman's perfume, but some men find it easier to inhale than the odor of a week old wound, or the foul smell of an unbathed, sweaty body.

Over on the Palm Beach side the scene was the same. A few more evening clothes, a few more diamonds; little more accent, a few more fakes. Over there a war was being fought from the wave washed sands of a placid resort. Over there too were men who know how war puts terror in timid hearts, but they were there not to talk about it. They had been in combat — with their draft boards. They had won. They had their stripes — deferment stripes. They were glad.

They said toasts to their stand-ins — the Yanks in the tanks.

They wondered when all the killing would be over and got drunk doing it.

Bill Herpel or Gordon Knight or Bradley O'Neal or John Carver probably could have answered their questions. But they were not there. Those boys and others like them will never be back to answer any questions. The last questions they answered were to God alone.

Bong. Bong. Bong.

The Old Year was dying.

At the fontalstones of time a New Year was being bathed in raw whiskey, imported liqueurs, and belly-washing gin.

Down at the foot of Clematis where Flagler Park splits the traffic, the signal lights blinked at names of boys probably dying too. But blood was substituted for liquor, soft prayers for drunken jargon and gray death for the rosy mists of life.

Other boys were being briefed in the ready room of death.

Thus on the last Sabbath night of the year, during the final tick-tocking moments of the hour, the Palm Beaches drank toasts to 1945 and braced themselves for battles ahead.

For this nation is at war.

CHAPTER 14

A Lost Soul on Enemy Soil

Karl Behrens was dead.

The young man, only eighteen, dangled from a tree, the rope from his own duffel bag taut around his neck. For him, World War II ended on the Lake Okeechobee dike—not far from the sugar fields where he and hundreds of German soldiers sat out the war in prisoner of war camps and where some of them died a long way from home.

You can still go to the spot where the camp stood, but you won't be able to find it. The buildings are long gone and the site has dissolved into the never-ending rows of cane. You can slog through the mud as Karl Behrens must have, feel the razor-sharp cane against your skin, watch with fear for the snakes or rats or alligators, as you make your way to the high dike surrounding the big lake. That's where Karl Behrens' young life ended.

Liberty Point operated near Clewiston from February 1944 to September 1945. The American Red Cross called the sweltering, dusty camp "the worst in all America." It and another camp in Belle Glade housed some 600 German soldiers. Local residents didn't particularly care to have the enemy so close, and the escapes, while few, were more than a little unsettling. That's why rumors flew that perhaps Karl Behrens had died at hands other than his own. Results of investigations, classified at the time and only recently obtained by the Palm Beach *Post* under the Freedom of Information Act, conclude he had not. How hard authorities tried to find out otherwise isn't evident in the documents and nearly all the people involved have long since died. But his brother, fifty years later, told of a somber nature and physical ills, circumstances that bolster a finding of suicide.

Ironically, Karl Behrens' demise may have been indirectly caused not by his American enemies but by his fellow Germans; their caste system offered little fondness for green recruits who went straight from the boot camp to the POW camp. Families of Americans who suffered or died at the hands of the Third Reich might be offended at the attention paid to a German soldier. But most can agree that wars are primarily the domain not of conquering generals, evil murderers or yellow cowards, but of scared young people doing their duty and suffering and bleeding and dying.

Stalag Florida

Karl Behrens was six feet tall, 150 lbs., with brown eyes, and light brown hair. Documents listed him as Protestant. He had fair skin. He was 18 years old. And he was a world away from home, a prisoner in a strange, hot place, where he would spend the last 4-1/2 months of his troubled and short life.

The Allied forces repossessing Europe had a problem—what to do with hordes of captured Germans. In May 1943, they began shipping captives over the Atlantic Ocean to the United States. Over the course of the war, nearly 378,000 German prisoners were housed at 666 different camps scattered across the country. More than 9,000 prisoners went to 22 Florida camps, many at or near military bases.

Robert Billinger, a professor at Wingate College near Charlotte, extensively researched the camps while a professor at Palm Beach Atlantic College in West Palm Beach. Eight were in North Florida and the Panhandle, seven in Central Florida and the Tampa Bay area, and five in southeast Florida. State headquarters was at Camp Blanding, between Jacksonville and Gainesville, also an active POW facility. It is now a National Guard training base.

But nothing remains of Liberty Point. Named for a fish camp that had once operated nearby, it was seven to nine miles west of Clewiston and a half-mile from Lake Okeechobee. Like its counterpart in Belle Glade, it was surrounded by fences and small guard towers. It sported white wooden barracks with green roofs and a recreation hall, theater, reading room and small infirmary.

The 200 to 300 prisoners got three uniforms and ate a healthy, if monotonous, fare. There were some luxuries; they saw films twice a week, assembled a concert band with instruments bought in West Palm Beach with money from their PX fund, and fished in nearby canals. The reading room featured American magazines and copies of the New York *Staatszeitung*—"state newspaper."

The prisoners also took advantage of classes in bookkeeping, English, geometry, chemistry. Some took advantage of religious activities. They played soccer and volleyball once a week at the school in Clewiston and at nearby Sugar Mill Park, and ping-pong with balls provided by a chaplain from West Palm Beach. The troops played soccer with British cadets training at nearby Riddle Field until the U.S. Army stopped the practice.

"The POW boys had a team that played softball against us at Clewiston's Sugarland Park," resident Bobby Hare recalled. "They'd have guards with them. Never had any problem with them. They were a fine bunch of regular guys."

But that was the extent of their leisure. Because the draft had decimated much of the American labor force and the war had disrupted the flow of Caribbean workers, the Germans were put to work performing the back-breaking sugar cane harvesting for which the Glades is infamous. The military charged farmers the going rate for the labor but were able to show a profit by paying the prisoners 80 cents a day in coupons they traded for items like cigarettes and beer, when available. Access to such treats led to a showdown with local distributors in early 1945. They halted supplies to Morrison Field, now Palm Beach International Airport, when they learned the facility was sharing them with the POWs.

"The 'hard core' Nazis who opted not to work were in camps in other parts of the country," Mary Krewson, whose husband, Tom Malone, was the camp's first sergeant, wrote in 1986. "Most of them spent a few cents for candy or cigarettes and saved most of what they earned, and it was banked for them and they took the funds with them when they were returned to Germany at the end of the war. They were very pleased at that because this money would go a long way in war-torn Germany."

Malone had a good relationship with the prisoners, Krewson wrote. Each morning, he would give the day's tasks to his counterpart among the prisoners, "and the German handled everything. They governed their own in day-to-day operations."

Malone wore no gun when he took them to Miami for medical treatment, Krewson wrote.

But the Germans had trouble with the tropical heat; every day after work guards loaded them in trucks and took them swimming in the big lake, she recalled.

"The time spent as POW wasn't that bad, especially since everything at home was going through turbulent times," former prisoner Josef Ebert wrote in June 1995. "We actually could sleep at night!"

Food was "OK," Ebert recalled. "We were never bored. On Sundays, we often received a big round cake since the sugar industry treated the camp to a whole sack of sugar. That was a nice gesture. We polished the floor in our chamber with liquid shoe paste by dancing around on it with old wool socks on our feet until the floor was shining. To add some flowers, we hung up a banana blossom in the middle of the room. It looked very nice."

Still, "sometimes I think of the snakes and alligators," he recalled.

"It might be that Liberty Point was the worst camp in the U.S. but it was not a total hell," former prisoner Josef Scholz wrote in August 1995. "We were POWs and not on vacation in Palm Beach or Miami!"

The camp "was desolate," Scholz said. "One camp street just went from one end to the other." The few showers were inadequate and toilets "catastrophic. Worms coming out of the sewers were crawling up on the walls, up to the seats of the toilets. It was best to use to the toilets at night, since then you couldn't see anything."

But he did say food was good and sufficient, treatment was fair "and sometimes more than understanding for our predicament" and "at the end, the war was over for us!"

Karl Baum, a prisoner at the camp from 1943 to 1946, who worked as a cook, called it "humane." Barracks, which held six men each, had mosquito netting but no air conditioning, Baum said. Prisoners went out before 8 a.m. and were back about 3 p.m. The American camp guards ate the same food as the soldiers, in keeping with the Geneva Convention. Prisoners weren't punished when they escaped.

Baum recalled only one incident; Germans had said they would not work the Monday after Easter, because that was a holiday back home.

"The captain came in and said, 'If you don't go to work, you don't eat.' That was the only punishment he gave us for not working."

Scholz said the only strike he recalled was for two days after prisoners were told to clear canals without protective leg gear and feared snakes and exposure to the foul water. The sugar firms eventually supplied the gear, Scholz said.

The Belle Glade camp operated from March to December 1945. Its occupants had picked oranges near Orlando before being transferred to the Glades. Despite encouragement from county agricultural agent "Red" Mounts — the son of local judge Marvin Mounts and the man for whom West Palm Beach's Mounts Botanical Garden is named — local farmers were hesitant to employ them. Two weeks after they arrived the Germans put Belle Glade on the national map when they held a two-day strike over a cut in cigarette rations. The American public, press and politicians, including U.S. Rep. Bob Sikes, D-Crestview, had a field day with this incident and others. They angrily painted word pictures of coddled Germans whining over cigarettes at a time when GIs were stumbling across the horrors that were the Nazi concentration camps. The strike was quickly put to an end. Thirty-nine prisoners considered troublemakers were transferred from Belle Glade to Camp Blanding. The army handed down a stern "no work, no eat" policy that allowed only bread and water for sloths.

"There was no one in Liberty Point who had any sympathy for this stupid strike," Liberty Point prisoner Josef Scholz said. He said he hopes the

39 "mischief makers" received "appropriate punishment."

Perhaps the greatest tragedy at Belle Glade came when two hot-dog British fliers from Riddle Field decided to buzz the camp in the dead of night. They made several runs and dives, then were unable to regain altitude and slammed into a nearby pasture. POWS recovered the bodies, which now lie at the famed British cemetery plot in Arcadia.

A patch of high dirt near the U.S. Agriculture Department's Belle Glade Experimental Station is the only evidence of the Belle Glade camp. Its flagpole now stands in front of Belle Glade's American Legion post.

At the Kendall camp in southern Dade County, then farmland and now a Metrorail station and barbecue restaurant a stone's throw from the sprawling Dadeland Mall, neighbors complained the Germans would throw "wolf whistles" their way.

On D-Day, the Miami *News* visited Clewiston, reporting the soldiers marched in from work in formation, their shovels slung over the shoulders like rifles. They'd heard of the invasion on radios bought with scrip. They believed the reports were propaganda and that Germany would surely prevail.

In March 1945, the American Red Cross inspected Liberty Point. The temperature hit 103 degrees and dust, aggravated by six months without rain, settled on everything. The Red Cross cited the camp for having only 12 latrines for 293 prisoners; only two had seats. It had three showers, one of which sometimes had hot water. Red Cross inspectors also worried about snakes. But the snakes should have been worried about the Germans, who converted them into belts and wallets. The team of inspectors found evidence prisoners were deliberately injuring themselves in hopes they would be transferred to northern camps with more hospital facilities.

Some prisoners had run out of patience and bolted for freedom, both at the Glades camps and the others in Florida. But Florida was not an easy place to be on the lam.

"They realized they had no place to go," recalled former U.S. Rep. Harry Johnston, D-West Palm Beach. He was 13 and 14 when he spent the summers of 1944 and 1945 manning a beer truck at the PX warehouse at Blanding, where Johnston's father was second in command.

Johnston recalled one escapee who got from North Florida all the way to the Everglades areas south of Lake Okeechobee that were not yet sugar fields.

"My father said, 'Let him go. He'll turn himself in,'" Johnston said. And the man did. He returned to the camp scratched, bloody and filthy. Johnston's father ordered the former fugitive paraded through Blanding's compound as a warning to the others. The head of the POWs complained.

"He said, 'You have violated the Geneva Convention. You've beaten this man,'" Johnston said. When the commander explained the Florida countryside, not the Army, had inflicted such punishment, the POW leader reportedly said, "God, it's hell out there. Don't escape."

But some ran anyway. One was Karl Behrens. By the time the Red Cross inspected Liberty Point, in March 1945, Karl was already dead.

Karl Behrens

Karl Behrens came from a city that was already seven centuries old when Europeans first came to Florida. Bremen, home to more than a half million people, lies forty-five miles south of the North Sea in northwestern Germany. It became an inland port when the Weser River was dredged; the prolific port, the first artificial harbor in Europe, and busy shipyards made Bremen an important German city — and an important target for any enemy. Between 1942 and 1945, Allied bombers destroyed 60 percent of the city.

About twelve miles north of downtown Bremen's historic Cathedral of St. Peter lies the suburb of Oberneuland, now a wealthy area of parks, quaint older villas and ornate mansions. Fifty years ago it was open country, dotted with farmhouses. The one at Hodenberger Deich 38 belonged to Heinrich Behrens. It was built in 1864 by Karl's great-grandfather. Heinrich kept a few pigs and cows to complement his regular job in a post office.

Karl, born May 11, 1926, was four years younger than his brother, Bernhard, and 11 years older than his sister, Martha.

Even two jobs weren't enough. Heinrich Behrens' wife and children worked every day after school and on weekends and holidays to feed the animals and help in the harvest.

Karl had a hard childhood, Bernhard said in a November 1993 interview conducted for the Palm Beach *Post* by reporter Hans-Peter Groth of Bremen's *Weser Kurier* newspaper.

Karl was a very shy child, often ill and subject to hyperactive, nervous behavior. And, his brother said, he had a low tolerance for heat.

When he turned six, Karl began an eight-year education in the Volksschule, Germany's primary school system. Then, only fourteen, he began an apprenticeship in a large repair shop for the Deutsche Reichsbahn, the national railroad company. By then, Germany was at war. On June 8, 1940, less than a month after his 14th birthday, the Royal Air Force had bombed Bremen.

Bernhard claimed his father was forced to join the Nazi party and was sent to war in 1939, just as Germany's campaign of conquest was beginning. After serving on the French front, he returned home, unscarred; the Army took into account his age and the needs of his farm, Bernhard said.

Karl and Bernhard, like many other German youngsters, had joined the Hitler Youth, an organization that involved 14-to-18-year-olds in various activities designed to further the Reich. Membership in the Youth had been mandatory since 1939. Bernhard insists the group was not a junior version of the feared Brown Shirts; it was more like a social club, an opportunity for fun in boring suburbia.

"We liked to do this," Bernhard said. "There was no other leisure activity besides Hitler Youth in Oberneuland. We had very nice uniforms and all our other friends were in the Hitler Youth."

"When they were children, teenagers and soldiers believed in Hitler and the Endsieg," the ultimate victory, Bernhard said. But he said his family would not describe themselves as "euphoric Nazis."

Three times in the summer of 1941, the RAF bombed Bremen; two runs were night raids. In 1942, Karl got his diploma as an engine fitter. After that, his brother said, he was forced to join the *Reichsarbeitsdienst*, a paramilitary labor battalion. He was sent to a lager—a camp—in a small town near Bremen and put to work in a swamp. His group also spent several days a week at a nearby airport, helping build and repair Focke Wulf storm fighter planes, designed to down bombers. Back home, his family had suffered a heavy RAF attack in September 1941; it was the 100th Allied raid on the town in the war. A year later on October 8, 1943, the U.S. 8th Air Force sent 357 bombers on a massive assault on Bremen and a nearby city. The Americans bombed Bremen again a week later. And on November 26, 663 American bombers bombarded the city; bad weather sharply limited damage.

In April 1944, Karl's labor battalion was ordered to the Western front in France. It was not integrated into the Wehrmacht, the German army, but went as a labor unit. It got special training and was deployed in an anti-aircraft battery mounted in a railroad wagon.

"Karl went into the war without fear," Bernhard said.

Bernhard later became a Luftwaffe radar operator in occupied Norway; after the Allies liberated that country he was interred by British troops before returning to Bremen at the end of the war.

One day, the Buergermeister of Oberneuland brought a letter to Hodenberger Deich 38. It was from the Wehrmacht. Karl had been captured.

The town of Cherbourg stands on the tip of the Cotentin peninsula, in the Normandy region of France, where Allied forces came ashore on D-Day, June 6, 1944. Taking Cherbourg, an important munitions-producing city, was a key goal for the Allies. Adolf Hitler had angrily dismissed a recommendation by Field Marshal Erwin Rommel to retreat from the peninsula, charging German forces at the Western front had been caught napping and accusing them of cowardice. He had ordered Cherbourg held "to the last man and the last bullet." But the advancing Allies had made their assault on the city June 18. Despite a request for surrender on June 21 and under a barrage of Allied artillery fire and air raids, the Germans had gamely fought on with what American correspondents called "the courage of despair." Some Germans, however, had quickly surrendered. On June 25, the head of the German garrison said his troopers were "worn out" and defeat inevitable, asking, "Is the sacrifice of the others still necessary?" Rommel had replied, "in accordance with the Fuehrer's orders, you are to hold out to the last round." American troops were already in the suburbs.

Finally, after 24 hours of house-to-house fighting, Cherbourg had fallen on June 26. Retreating Germans torched an aircraft factory and the port. The city was a smoking ruin. Some 25,000 prisoners were captured. One was Karl Behrens, taken by the U.S. Army on June 27. The family never learned the circumstances, Bernhard Behrens said. Later, Karl's parents received a letter from him. He was in a prison camp in Florida. He had arrived July 19 at Camp Blanding, and been transferred to Liberty Point on August 16. His parents were glad he'd been captured by the Americans, who they believed would treat German prisoners more humanely than others. Karl wrote a few times during his incarceration, describing hard labor in the sugar fields. But, Bernhard said, "he gave the impression that everything was all right with him and he felt OK."

Tensions in Camp

The record of life inside the German POW camps would hint Karl was anything but OK. Tension between Germans and Americans may have been only a minor problem compared to the apparent acrimony within the ranks of the Reich. German prisoners of war set up their own social structure, loosely split into three groups, with declining social rank. First came the Afrika Korps, Rommel's elite tank corps, captured during America's initial involvement in the war, the North Africa campaign in 1942. Next were the troops seized in late 1943 and 1944 in Italy, the first stop in the Allied recapture of Europe. The last group comprised those captured after D-Day, June 6, 1944. Most of them were relatively new recruits. Many had been pulled from their farms. Some were extremely young. A desperate Germany was starting to throw every body it could find at the Allied juggernaut.

The Afrika Korps had been among the Fuehrer's finest, smartest, fittest and most loyal troops.

"They trusted me because I was a young kid," Harry Johnston recalled. "They promised me 'inside work' after the war. There was no question in their mind that the Germans were going to win."

When the Italian campaign detainees arrived, the Korps POWs refused to believe the Allies had taken Italy, Johnston said. And when those captured after D-Day came in, Johnston said, the Korps officers concluded they were spies who were lying to them about the Normandy Invasion, "that we could never cross the channel from Europe to England. They believed first they (the latest arrivals) were lower class and second (that) they were spies, that they were put in there to demoralize them."

Former prisoner Josef Scholz said he never saw veteran prisoners harass newcomers and that by then, "only a few still believed that Germany was going to win the war."

Among those later arrivals at Clewiston, in the summer of 1944, was a lanky private named Karl Behrens. He was assigned POW number 208541.

The Korps prisoners lorded over the others, meting out discipline and punishment.

"It was terrible," Harry Johnston recalled of the situation at Blanding. "They were beaten up. In fact my father had to separate them in barracks eventually."

Roberta Avant, a clerk at the U.S. Army Corps of Engineers office in Clewiston, was twice called to Liberty Point to accompany investigating officers and take testimony after prisoners had died.

"Some of the men were very brutal and attacked the mild-mannered ones," Avant, who still lives in Clewiston, recalled. She said prisoners were often in fights, even though they were heavily guarded. Once, a man was smothered in his own bed, Avant said. None of the other men in the small cabin reported hearing a sound or movement. Although it might have happened, the spotty records connected with the camp don't show such a death.

Ex-prisoner Karl Baum grew up in a part of Czechoslovakia inhabited by ethnic Germans and called the Sudetenland, one of the first areas seized by Hitler. After the war, he applied for U.S. citizenship. He now lives in California; his son lives in Boynton Beach. Baum, who was in the Afrika Korps, denied his group mistreated the other German prisoners.

"We only know that they were from the last phase of the war," he said. "We didn't have nothing against them."

But Roberta Avant said she sometimes wondered if escapees were fleeing other prisoners rather than the American authorities.

Just months after arriving at Liberty Point, Karl Behrens escaped.

The Escape

About 5:30 p.m. on December 30, 1944 — a Saturday — a German company leader told a U.S. sergeant that Karl Behrens had not reported back to camp after working in the sugar fields since 3:00 p.m. with Work Group 2. A group of twenty-five prisoners had been cutting weeds and clearing a canal along a lane cut between two 40-acre plots of cane. They were split into three groups; two went off for other jobs and the one containing Behrens stayed. The group leader was about to send Behrens off when Karl begged off, saying he had almost finished his work and was tired. The leader said he saw Behrens sit down to rest about 2 p.m. The sergeant and two Germans went to where Karl had been working — about a quarter mile west and a half-mile north of the camp — but didn't find him. They first supposed he had gone to wash himself in a canal or take a snooze in a cane field. They returned to camp, checked his bunk and found some items missing. They scoured the area around the camp and again searched where Karl had been working, without result. Around 9 p.m., the commander called the FBI.

The FBI's report of Karl's escape and death was provided to the Palm Beach *Post* under the federal Freedom of Information Act.

Hugh MacMillan, resident agent in the FBI's West Palm Beach office, had just come from searching trains and planes for a German agent suspected to be in the area and had just been notified that man had been caught in New York. Now he had an escaped prisoner in his area. MacMillan had been in the FBI since 1940 and had become a resident agent in West Palm Beach just that year.

"We had a meeting and fanned out," MacMillan — later a Palm Beach Circuit Court Judge and the father of the former Palm Beach County School Board member of the same name — recalled in a 1993 interview. He died March 18, 1995.

MacMillan, along with West Palm Beach agents George Brouillard and Jack Borden and Fort Myers agent John Loome, arrived at 11 o'clock that night. They immediately joined the search, along with two Clewiston officers, a Hendry County deputy, a constable from Belle Glade, and three Highway Patrol officers from Pahokee, Belle Glade and Fort Myers. A lieutenant from Liberty Point had also assembled a detail of six men to patrol strategic points on roads and highways leading to the camp and to the Lake Okeechobee dike. Urgent teletypes were sent to FBI offices in

Atlanta, Savannah, Georgia, and Birmingham, Alabama; to Army officials in Atlanta and Navy authorities in Charleston, South Carolina. Local authorities and the press were notified. Roads were blocked and cars searched, the Clewiston *News* reported.

"War Prisoner Hunted in Glades," the Miami *Herald* said in a brief story at the bottom of its front page, accompanied by a mug shot of a grim looking Behrens. The Palm Beach *Post* also reported the escape in a front-page brief.

Two more FBI agents joined the search the next day, New Year's Eve. MacMillan recalled all-night searches through dense lakeshore vegetation and jagged pieces of cut cane.

"Have you ever tried to walk through sugar cane?" MacMillan said. "It's like a jungle."

In his diary, still in his possession years later, MacMillan wrote that he was up for forty hours, scouring the countryside in the bitter cold with the other officers, alerting service station operators, even looking under the 20 Mile Bend bridge, halfway between West Palm Beach and Belle Glade. He warmed himself at the Clewiston Inn fireplace. Meanwhile, authorities quizzed fellow POWs who had been close with Behrens. One said he didn't know of Behrens' escape plans and believed he may have gone to sleep in the field. He said other members of the work group said Karl liked to swim and suggested he may have left the field to take a swim in a nearby canal and drowned. The group leader said Behrens spoke no English. He said Behrens was quiet and in good health and was a good worker. He said he believed Behrens had had some sort of accident rather than trying to escape. The group leader said that, since he'd arrived, Karl hadn't received a single piece of mail. One who was from the same part of Germany as Karl described the 18-year-old as being almost childish. He also said he knew of no escape plans and believed Karl had had an accident.

Other prisoners described Karl as moody and quiet and said he hadn't any close friends at the camp. An American private who helped translate interviews said the prisoners indicated Karl was despondent and he believed they were sincere when they said he had not planned his escape.

In his bunk, authorities found 4-1/2 coupon booklets and an undated letter in German addressed "Lieber Karl" — Dear Karl — and signed "the Christmas man." The FBI report said the letter was unintelligible.

Authorities first said a khaki raincoat, pants, a khaki shirt and a blue denim work jacket were missing, but they were later found where Karl had left them hanging in another barracks. They did find that the sash cord from Karl's duffel bag had been removed.

A news report said agents dismissed a theory he'd been the victim of other prisoners because he was anti-Nazi. They did say he'd received no news from home since his capture.

"He was a young fellow," former fellow prisoner Karl Baum said. "He was very quiet. I could never understand. He didn't look to me to be the time to ever escape. He didn't stand out, not in sports. You couldn't see much difference there...He couldn't cope maybe with the weather."

"He just left and that's it. There was plenty of opportunities. But where would we go? There was no way not to be caught. From Clewiston it would be 80 miles before you get to a beach. It was surrounded by sugar fields and swamp. We get so used to it. There was not a day (that) at least two or three rattlesnakes was (not) caught. There was no place to go. You would only escape and get caught again."

As the search continued, a man staying at a New York hotel penned a letter January 2 to the head of the FBI. The man, whose name is blacked out in the FBI's report, wrote that just before 11:00 a.m. the previous Tuesday, December 26, he was boarding a subway train to see his lawyer when he saw a slender youth, about 18.

"His stance standing in front of a door told me at once that boy had been in training under the Nazi," wrote the man, who said he'd seen such postures during a visit to Germany in 1937. He said the young man had "that certain look that never fails — perhaps you would call it hunted."

The writer said he didn't think about the mysterious man again until he heard radio commentator Walter Winchell mention Karl's escape on his nationwide Sunday night broadcast December 31. He said the young man he saw "could easily" fit Karl's description. The writer said he contacted the FBI's New York office and was told an agent would see him. He said no one had shown but perhaps that was because he had given no name, just his room number at the Roosevelt Hilton, at Madison Avenue and 45th Street in Manhattan. The man said if it wasn't Karl, it may well have been another Nazi, but he asked agents to come with pictures of the men the Feds were looking for. He said friends would attest that "I never forget a face." He concluded by asking his letter not be kept in files, then added a postscript that a mountain range near the Hudson Valley "would be a perfect hideaway for those we do not wish in this country."

A January 9 return letter signed by Hoover said, "It was indeed kind of you to bring this information to my attention." The agency had apparently opted not to give the man the bad news that Karl Behrens had escaped four days after the businessman saw the mysterious youth on the New York subway. Instead it just told him the search for Karl Behrens was already over.

Karl Found

MacMillan looked for Behrens for two days before finding him hanging from a banyan tree, about two miles northwest of the camp and about seventy-five yards south of the Lake Okeechobee dike, according to the FBI report.

On New Year's Day, MacMillan got the key to the gate at the Lake Okeechobee levee and rode his 1941 Chevrolet up to the top of the tall dike. He was wondering if Behrens had been despondent and thrown himself into the lake or a rim canal.

"I looked over to my left and saw the body hanging under a small tree," MacMillan said. "I was distressed that he hanged himself. But the problem of his escape had been solved, and that was the end of that particular sentiment."

The wind twisted his body. It had been well concealed by the branches. His feet were about a foot off the ground. He was dressed in his POW garb, blue denim shirt and pants, as well as brown shorts. The back of his neck was swollen and waxen. His head tilted forward. He hung by a doubled sash cord about two feet long, tied at the back of his neck. A military belt of heavy cloth was looped around the limb near the cord, and authorities speculate he used the belt to position himself for his suicide. Two large branches near the ground had been hacked and broken off to clear a space for his body to hang. The report said there was no evidence of a struggle. About fifteen yards away, the searchers found Karl's hoe propped by rocks; over the handle was his blue denim hat, his gloves, a jackknife and his glasses in a metal case. Wood splinters clung to the knife blade. Standing near the body, under an overcast sky, the camp sergeant snapped several photographs, most of which were very dark. The pictures were sent to various agencies. MacMillan kept a shot he had made with his own Polaroid.

After his body was taken down, camp physician Captain J.E. Long of the Medical Corps inspected it. He reported finding no signs of violence. Long told investigators the condition of the body led him to conclude Karl died forty-eight hours earlier — on December 30, the day he escaped. Long lists cause of death on Behrens' death certificate as "strangulation self-inflicted by hanging." A later autopsy, conducted at Camp Blanding, agreed.

The Army notified the Germans through the Swiss embassy in Washington. Stories of Karl's death ran in local newspapers and by wire service around the country.

"Behrens left no note," Hugh MacMillan's boss, R.G. Danner, special agent in charge of the Miami office, declared, "but all surrounding circumstances indicated that he had taken his own life."

The FBI, the military and the Security Intelligence Division all concluded Karl Behrens' death was a suicide. The FBI's seven-page report, completed February 9, 1945, ended with the notation, "CLOSED."

Back Home in Bremen

It was the mayor of Oberneuland who came to the Behrens home with "the awful news," Bernhard Behrens said. But the family had little time to grieve. The Allies were coming. In April 1945, the British began pushing toward Bremen. By April 26, the Allies controlled the city. Bremen had been devastated by the war, but Oberneuland, about 12 miles north of downtown, had been spared serious damage. After the war, the United States used Bremen as a port for supplying war-ravaged Europe.

"During this time, many of us thought very friendly about the U.S. military," Bernhard said.

Meanwhile, the family was coping with Karl's suicide. They didn't have to look far to solve the mystery. Karl had come from what would fifty years later be called a dysfunctional family. Several times in the 1930s, his father had tried to kill himself, Bernhard said. He said he suspects Karl never got over the shock. He said Karl suffered from depression and had difficulty dealing with the hard labor. And South Florida was the last place to send someone with a low tolerance for heat. All of this, plus homesickness, probably led Karl to suicide, Bernhard said.

The family never pressed for more about Karl's escape and death and never tried to return his body, Bernhard said. It wasn't until the 1950s that the family found where he was buried. An officer who had been in Florida sent pictures of his grave. No one in the family has ever come to the United States.

Routed By Nature

Karl Behrens' escape was not the last from Liberty Point. Two more prisoners fled January 23 and were picked up early January 25 by a deputy, a game warden, and a U.S. Navy firemen on leave. The three were searching for game law violators when they found the Germans on a highway near Palmdale. Planes from the Riddle Field training airfield in Clewiston had also searched from the air. Glades area residents had been instructed to strip laundry from clotheslines before nightfall so escapees wouldn't steal clothes.

Wilhem Stuttgen and Gerhard Anklam said they had planned to stow aboard a ship at Jacksonville. When captured, the two carried toilet articles and drinking water and were still wearing their "PC" uniforms. There was good reason; dressed in civilian clothes, the escaped Germans could be treated as spies and face criminal sanctions that included long prison terms and death.

"Wilhem Stuttgen and I saw a reason, as Karl Behrens probably did, to leave in the terrible treatment of the POW's by the camp commander," Gerhard Anklam wrote in May 1994. "This Captain Dwight Field, a German hater, demanded under the most adverse climatic conditions ever more productivity in the sugar cane fields."

Former prisoner Josef Scholz said Field was fair. He said prisoners were allowed pets and Field ordered up a truckload of beer for Christmas 1944. Scholz said escape from Liberty Point was relatively easy and prisoners would keep it quiet for several days, "but to where and why?"

At Liberty Point, the escapes soon faded into memories, fears of sabotage declined, and conditions became more informal. The monotony of camp life was broken up only by mail trucks from Camp Blanding or visits from area bases. Finally, it was the forces of nature that shut down the Clewiston camp. Already scheduled to be phased out in September 1945, the sugar crops' cultivation work done for the growing season, it was hurriedly evacuated as a hurricane threatened South Florida. Ironically, prisoners sent by train to Camp Blanding steered right into the storm, which tormented the railroad cars with buffeting winds and driving rains. The trains finally arrived in North Florida and deposited wet and exhausted guards and POWS, who promptly brawled with their respective counterparts at Camp Blanding. Furious commanders first ordered everyone to walk all the way back to Clewiston, then backed off. Several weeks later, the POWs were transferred to North Florida. The Blanding POW camp was disbanded in early 1946. The Belle Glade camp stayed open until December 1945.

All German prisoners were eventually repatriated, except those who had died.

The day after Karl Behrens was found dead, Sea Shole Funeral Home in Jacksonville brought his body to Camp Blanding. His was grave 2 of a series of plots for POWs who died in Florida. The army paid the undertaker $95: $25 for embalming, $10 for hearse service and $60 for the casket in which Karl was laid to rest on January 5, 1945. No headstone was authorized. In April 1946, his body was moved to a special cemetery for German POWs at Fort Benning in Columbus, Georgia. He lies there today, at section A-2, Grave 189.

Bernhard Behrens, now in his 70s, retired in 1985 after years as a clerk in a company that distributes paint tinting. He has spent his free time as president of a soccer club for four decades. Bernhard said he has few memories of his brother. Bernhard's sister, Martha, still lives in Bremen. But their parents have been dead for years. The animals are long gone, the farmland sold off. Bernhard and his wife still live in the house at Hodenberger Deich 38.

Hanging in the living room of the home are several family pictures. One shows Karl and Bernhard as young boys. Another is Karl in his uniform, his youth frozen forever.

German Prisoner Camps in Florida

1. Eglin Field
2. Camp Gordon Johnston
3. Telogia
4. Dale Mabry Field, near Tallahassee
5. White Springs
6. Camp Blanding
7. Hastings
8. DeLand
9. Leesburg
10. Dade City
11. Drew Field, now Tampa International Airport
12. MacDill Field, now MacDill Air Force Base, Tampa
13. Orlando
14. Winter Haven
15. Venice
16. Liberty Point, near Clewiston
17. Belle Glade
18. Belle Haven
19. Kendall
20. Homestead

POW CAMPS IN FLORIDA

During World War II, more than 9,000 prisoners went to 22 Florida camps, many at or near military bases.

1. Eglin Field
2. Camp Gordon Johnson
3. Telogia
4. Dale Mabry Field
5. White Springs
6. Camp Blanding
7. Green Cove Springs
8. Hastings
9. DeLand
10. Leesburg
11. Dade City
12. Drew Field
13. MacDill Field
14. Orlando
15. Winter Haven
16. Venice
17. Liberty Point
18. Belle Glade
19. Belle Haven
20. Page Field
21. Kendall
22. Homestead

STAFF GRAPHIC

Source: Palm Beach *Post*, Camp Blanding Museum,
the Florida Historical Society

Karl Behrens' official "mug shots" from the FBI file on his escape and death. (Photo courtesy of the Federal Bureau of Investigation)

This picture of Karl Behrens is in his former home near Bremen, Germany. (Photo courtesy of Jochen Stoss)

Acknowledgements & Sources

This book is by no means a comprehensive overview of the World War II experience in Florida. Suggested works for additional reading:

Wynne, Lewis N, editor, *Florida at War*; 1993, St. Leo, Fla., St. Leo Press

Mormino, Gary Ross, *War Clouds and the Sunshine State: World War Two and Florida*; 1998, Tampa, University of South Florida.

Most of these segments were adapted from stories published between 1991 and 1995 in the Palm Beach *Post*, which has graciously given permission for their adaptation and republication. *Post* archives have supplied many of the photographs. Special thanks to Managing Editor Tom O'Hara, Editor Edward Sears, and Associate Editor Jan Tuckwood, and Arnold Rosenfeld, senior vice president for Cox Newspapers. They envisioned the 5-year project, encouraged my ideas and made sure my stories were presented in beautiful layouts with dramatic photographs and graphics, created or assembled by the *Post*'s talented staff. Howard Kleinberg, a newspaper veteran of nearly a half century who, at thirteen, watched the Pacific Fleet parade triumphantly down New York's Hudson River, provided invaluable editing suggestions and caught more than one spelling or fact error. And my wife, Debra, and sons Robert and Henry tolerated me, which may have been the greatest gift.

Because these were originally newspaper articles, sources of information are those quoted or cited directly in the text. Special sources and contributors for segments, as well as the date the original article appeared in the *Post*, are listed below.

Chapter I
Three Florida Boys at Pearl

Originally appeared December 7, 1991.

Sources:

The families, friends and fellow servicemen of Ralph Hollis, Claude Edward Rich and Eugene V. Lish

The archives of the Palm Beach *Post*

The courts, school boards, historical societies, libraries and American Legion and Veterans of   Foreign Wars posts of Palm Beach and St. Lucie counties

The Palm Beach High School Historical Committee
The United States Naval Institute and the Naval Historical Center
The *USS Arizona* Memorial
The Pearl Harbor Survivors Association; Pearl Harbor History Associates Inc., and Pearl Harbor historians Jim Blach and Ray Emory

Chapter II
The War Offshore
Originally appeared February 16, 1992
Sources:
Historical Societies of Florida, South Florida, Palm Beach, Martin and St. Lucie counties, Boca Raton and Jupiter
Archives of the U.S. Navy and U.S. Coast Guard
National Archives
Florida historians Bessie DuBois, Michael Gannon and Rody Johnson
North Carolina historian Paul Branch
Tebeau, Charlton, *A History of Florida,* 1971, Coral Gables, University of Miami Press
Gannon, Michael, *Operation Drumbeat,* 1991, New York, Harper & Row
Mandano, Mark, *A Divers Guide to Shipwrecks: Cape Canaveral to Jupiter Light,* 1992, Vero Beach, self-published

Chapter III
Bread Wrappers and Theater Tickets
Originally appeared February 16, 1992
Sources:
Same as for *The War Offshore*

Chapter IV
The Invasion of Florida
Written for this publication
Sources:
Prior, Leon O., "Nazi Invasion of Florida!" *Florida Historical Quarterly* (October 1970.) Prior   was an FBI agent assigned to the case
Glover, Charles E., Palm Beach Post-Cox News Service, "Six German Saboteurs Executed by Army," Palm Beach *Post*, August 9, 1992
Dasch, Georg Johann, *Eight Spies Against America*, 1959, New York, R.M. McBride Co.
"Is This Nazi Secret Agent Telling the Truth?" *Newsweek*, November 30, 1959, page 29.

"Notorious Offender" files, U.S. Bureau of Prisons. From National Archives, Textual Reference Branch; courtesy Archives researcher Fred J. Romanski, October 1995.

Cirino, Paul, "Stolen History Marker Recovered," *Florida Times-Union*, July 12, 1991, page B-5

Hogencamp, Kevin, "Nazis On Our Soil," *Florida Times-Union*, June 16, 1992, page A-1, A-6

Letter from German Archives, Aachen, Germany; January 26, 1996

Letters from city officials of Ludwigshafen, Germany; December 11, 1995 and June 3, 1996

Chapter V
The Military Bases

Adapted from stories which appeared December 9, 1989, February 16, 1992, and October 10. 1993. Palm Beach *Post* Staff Writer Carolyn Fretz contributed

Sources:

Florida military historian Robert Hawk

Jupiter historian Bessie DuBois

Officials of Jonathan Dickinson State Park, Palm Beach International Airport and Boca Raton Municipal Airport

Historical societies of Palm Beach and Martin counties and Boca Raton

The archives of the Palm Beach *Post*

Chapter VI
The Medal Bill Murden Never Got

Written for this publication.

Sources:

Correspondence from William J. Murden to Boca Raton Historical Society, date unknown; to author, May 14, 1993.

Telephone conversation with Gladys Murden, November 25, 1998

Peekskill (N.Y.) Herald, November 3 and November 5, 1998

The Transmitter, newsletter of Boca Raton Army Air Field, February 28, 1993.

Chapter VII
A Little Corner of England in the Florida Scrub

Originally appeared May 31, 1988, June 21, 1994. Palm Beach *Post* photographer Robert Shanley contributed.

Sources:

Rotary Club of Arcadia
K-Post 11 American Legion Auxiliary, Arcadia
Oak Ridge Cemetery, Arcadia
DeSoto County Chamber of Commerce
Clewiston Museum
Historical Branch, British Air Ministry, London
Morgan, Hugh, *By the Seat of Your Pants!* 1990, Kent, England, Newton
    Publishers

Chapter VIII
"An Abominable Situation:" Black Exploitation in the War Effort
Originally appeared August 23, 1992
Sources:
    Palm Beach *Post* editorial writer Stebbins Jefferson, niece of Charles
        Stebbins Jr.
    Educator Ineria Hudnell
    The Florida Historical Society
    The archives of the Palm Beach *Post*
    Rouson-Gossett, Vivian Reissland; Pompey, C. Spencer, eds., *Like A
        Mighty Banyan: Contributions of Black People to the History of Palm Beach
        County*, 1982, West Palm Beach, Palm Beach Junior College

Chapter IX
How Did My Brother Die?
Originally appeared May 31, 1992
Sources:
    Kay Brainard Hutchins
    Kassel Mission Memorial Association
    The 8th Air Force News
    The National Archives
    Archives of the Palm Beach *Post*
    Gunter Lemke and Walter Hassenpflug, Bad Hersfeld, Germany

Chapter X
Shooting Stars and Friendly Fire
Originally appeared August 6, 1994
    Shannon Johnson of the Palm Beach *Post* Washington bureau and
        reporter Wayne Linke of the De Funiak Springs *Herald-Breeze* contrib-
        uted
Sources:
    David Cosson, Wallace Cosson and Robert Mickler

Former U.S. Rep. Earl Hutto

National Archives and archives of U.S. Army, U.S. Air Force and Eglin Air Force Base

Congressional Record

Linke, Wayne, "Family Remembers Bombs of Death," De Funiak Springs *Herald-Breeze*, August 16, 1993.

Chapter XI
The Day They Bombed Frostproof

Originally appeared August 6, 1994

Sources:

Virginia Lyle, Dr. Kenneth Dunham

Kathleen L. Ellis, secretary, Frostproof Historical Society

Air Force Archives, Maxwell Air Force Base, Ala.

National Archives

U.S. Air Force, Avon Park Bombing Range, MacDill Air Force Base

U.S. Court of Claims

Highland News, Lake Wales *Highlander*, Lakeland *Ledger*, Tampa *Tribune*; August 23, August 24, August 25, 1944

Chapter XII
A Meeting at Cap's Place

Written for this publication

Sources:

Rodney Dillon, Broward County Historical Commission

Weidling, Philip, "Biggest Story `Blacked Out' in Broward," Miami *Herald*, June 29, 1961.

Tusa, Rosa, "Cap's Place: Good Food in a Down South Atmosphere," Palm Beach *Post*, August 22, 1980, page B-1.

Cruickshank, Ken, "Taking a boat ride into the Weatherbeaten Past," Palm Beach *Post*, July 2, 1982

Marbella, Jean, "Legendary Longer Gets New Complex," Fort Lauderdale *Sun-Sentinel*, June 6, 1982

"Woman of the Year: Mrs. Wallis Warfield Simpson," *Time*, Jan 4, 1937

Dieterich, Emily Perry, and Jane S. Day, Research Atlantica, Inc., "Cap's Place: A Nomination to the National Register to Historic Places," prepared for the Hasis family, owners of Cap's Place, November 1989.

Dieterich, Emily Perry, "Welcome to Cap's Place," *South Florida History Magazine*, Historical Association of South Florida, Spring 1990

Gilbert, Martin, *Churchill: A Life*; *Winston S. Churchill: Road to Victory, 1941-1945*, 1986; all New York, Houghton Mifflin

Churchill, Winston S., *The Grand Alliance*, 1950, New York, Houghton Mifflin

Wilson, Charles (Lord Moran,) *Churchill: the Struggle for Survival, 1940-1965, Taken from the Diaries of Lord Moran*, 1966, New York, Houghton Mifflin

Letter from Martin Gilbert, London, February 8, 1995

Letters from Raymond Teichman, supervisory archivist, Franklin D. Roosevelt Presidential Library, Hyde Park, N.Y.; August 23 and September 7, 1995

Letter from Thomas E. Camden, Director for Library & Archives and Curator of Collections, George C. Marshall Foundation, Lexington, Va.; November 1, 1995.

Letter from Richard M. Langworth, President, International Churchill Society of the United States, Hopkinton, N.H.; August 25, 1995.

Letter from Robert P. Richardson, Freedom of Information Act liaison, U.S. Department of Defense Intelligence Agency; October 30, 1995.

Chapter XIII
A Little Too Close to Home
Compiled for this publication

Chapter XIV
Another Lost Soul on Enemy Soil
Originally appeared December 28, 1994

Palm Beach *Post* Staff Writer Viola Geinger and executive secretary Barbara Palmowski and Cox Newspapers London Bureau Chief Lou Salome contributed

Hans-Peter Groth, staff writer, *Weser Kurier* newspaper and Jochen Stoss, freelance photographer, both of Bremen, Germany, contributed

Sources:
Bernhard Behrens
Robert D. Billinger Jr., Wingate College, Wingate, N.C.
Dr. Arnold Krammer, History Department, Texas A&M University
George Cordes, Clewiston Museum
Bobby N. Hare, Clewiston
Dick Blackwell, Chief Deputy Clerk of Glades County Court, Moore Haven

Former POWs Gerhard Anklam, Josef Ebert, Josef Scholz and Karl Baum

David Coles, Florida Archives

Ken Schlesinger, Military Reference Branch, National Archives

Carl Cocke, U.S. Center for Military History

Federal Bureau of Investigation

Deutsche Dienststelle (German archives), Berlin, Germany

Bundesarchiv, Militararchive, Aachen, Germany

German War Graves Commission, Kassel, Germany

Camp Blanding (Fla.) and Fort Benning (Ga.) museums

Palm Beach County, South Florida and Florida historical societies

Archives of the Palm Beach *Post* and Palm Beach *Times*, Miami *Herald*, Miami *News* and Clewiston *News*

Billinger, Robert, "With the Wehrmacht in Florida: The German POW Facility at Camp Blanding, 1942-1946." *Florida Historical Quarterly*, 1979

Salmaggi, Cesare; Pallavisini, Alfredo; eds, *2194 Days of War: An Illustrated Chronology of the Second World War*, 1979, New York, Mayflower Books

Shirer, William R., *The Rise and Fall of the Third Reich*, 1960, New York, Simon and Schuster

Also by Eliot Kleinberg
- *Pioneers in Paradise: West Palm Beach, The First Hundred Years* (with Jan Tuckwood), 1994
- *Florida Fun Facts: 1,001 Fun Questions and Answers About Florida,* 1995
- *The Historical Traveler's Guide to Florida,* 1997
- *Weird Florida,* 1998
- *Our Century,*the Palm Beach *Post's* special section on Palm Beach County and the Treasure Coast in the 20th Century (2000)(Primary writer)
- *Black Cloud,* a 75th anniversary book on the great 1928 Okeechobee Hurricane, 2003.
- *Weird Florida II: In a State of Shock,* 2005
- *Florida Hurricane and Disaster, 1992,* his father's memoir of his family's ordeal in Hurricane Andrew (1993)(Contributor)

About the author:

Eliot Kleinberg was born in Coral Gables in 1956, graduated the Miami-area public schools in 1974, and received two degrees from the University of Florida.